Capital and Communities
in Black and White

SUNY Series: The New Inequalities
A. Gary Dworkin, editor

Capital and Communities in Black and White

The Intersections of Race, Class, and Uneven Development

Gregory D. Squires

State University of New York Press

Published by
State University of New York Press, Albany

For information, address State University of New York Press,
State University Plaza, Albany, NY 12246

Production by Christine Lynch
Marketing by Nancy Farrell

Library of Congress Cataloging-in-Publication Data

Squires, Gregory D.
    Capital and communities in black and white : the intersections of
race, class, and uneven development / by Gregory D. Squires.
        p.   cm. — (SUNY series, the new inequalities)
    Includes bibliographical references and index.
    ISBN 0–7914–1987–8 (alk. paper). — ISBN 0–7914–1988–6 (pbk. :
alk. paper)
        1. Urban renewal—United States. 2. United States—Race
relations. 3. Urban policy—United States. 4. Community
development, Urban—United States. 5. United States—Economic
policy. I. Title. II. Series.
HT175.S68   1994
307.3'46'0973—dc20   93–30567
                                                                              CIP

10 9 8 7 6 5 4 3 2

Contents

Acknowledgments

Several people and organizations have provided invaluable support—financial, intellectual, and other—over the years that it has taken to complete this book. Many invaluable debts are too numerous to name here, but they are noted in the citations on the following pages. Some people have been particularly helpful in keeping me focused on the scholarly paths I attempted to follow and the concrete realities of urban life to which I have tried to respond. Joe Feagin, William J. Wilson, Gale Cincotta, and, closer to home, Bill Velez and Joan Moore, my colleagues in the Department of Sociology at the University of Wisconsin–Milwaukee, Dan Willett, Executive Director of the Fair Lending Coalition in Milwaukee, and Bill Tisdale and Carla Wertheim with the Metropolitan Milwaukee Fair Housing Council, have been most helpful in these regards.

My wife, Margot, and children, Erin and Ian, have been most tolerant of the time and energy this has taken. (Indeed, sometimes I think my daughter and son like the distractions from what they believe to be my over-protective style of parenting.) Without their daily presence and support, this book would never have been written.

Assistance has also been provided by several organizations including the City of Milwaukee, the Milwaukee Foundation, the University of Wisconsin System Institute on Race and Ethnicity, as well as the Social Science Research Facility, the Urban Research Center, and the Urban Studies Programs at the University of Wisconsin–Milwaukee.

Some of the chapters in this book are revisions of previously published papers. I want to thank the publishers for allowing me to use the following materials.

"Deindustrialization, Economic Democracy, and Equal Opportunity: The Changing Context of Race Relations in Urban America," in Michael Peter Smith (ed.), *Breaking Chains, Comparative Urban and Community Research*, volume 3 (New Brunswick: Transaction Publishers, 1991).

"The Political Economy of Housing: All the Discomforts of Home," in Ray Hutchison (ed.), *New Perspectives in Urban Sociology: Research in Urban Sociology*, volume 3 (Greenwich, CT.: JAI Press, 1993).

"Community Reinvestment: The Privatization of Fair Lending Law Enforcement," in Robert D. Bullard, Charles Lee, and Eugene Grigsby (eds.), *Residential Apartheid: The American Legacy* (Los Angeles: UCLA Center for Afro-American Studies, 1994).

"Partnership and the Pursuit of the Private City," in Mark Gottdiener and Chris G. Pickvance (ed.), *Urban Life in Transition, Urban Affairs Annual Reviews*, volume 39 (Newbury Park, CA: Sage Publications, 1991). ©1991. Reprinted by permission of Sage Publications, Inc.

1

Restructuring, Place, and Race: An Introduction

> I think it might be good that the disturbances or
> riots took place in Los Angeles. It woke up Amer-
> ica to the fact that there are two Americas. . . . We
> have slowly but surely built two New Yorks, two
> Washingtons, two Los Angeleses, two Atlantas.
> And quite often, they don't even know each other.
>
> Jimmy Carter, 1992

Bernhard Goetz shoots four black youths in a New York subway car in 1984 and is hailed a hero by many, blacks in the Overtown neighborhood of Miami set property on fire and clash with police on three separate occasions threatening postponement of the Super Bowl in 1989, Rodney King's beating by Los Angeles police in 1991 is captured on videotape for the entire nation to see, and incidents of racial violence continue to explode across urban America. After declining steadily for at least thirty-five years, poverty begins rising again in the mid 1970s, a so-called underclass emerges in the bowels of urban America capturing the attention of journalists, scholars, policymakers, and the general public while glittering office towers, luxury hotels, mega-malls, and entertainment centers mushroom in downtown central business districts and suburban communities. Japan and Germany, if not Asia and Europe generally, emerge as powerful international trade blocks while the United States loses hundreds of thousands of manufacturing jobs, and although productivity increases, income goes down.

These seemingly disparate social phenomena are in fact closely intertwined. If the color line proved to be the problem of the twentieth century as W. E. B. DuBois forewarned ninety years ago (DuBois 1965, 239), it appears the same could reasonably be predicted for the twenty-first. But to understand the dynamics of race today requires coming to terms with the dramatic restructuring of the U.S. economy and spatial redevelopment of metropolitan areas that has taken place in the post–World War II years and continues apace today. These structural, spatial, and social developments are pieces of a broader process of uneven development. None of these trajectories of change can be understood in isolation. Each of them affects, and is intricately affected by, the others. Tracing these developments and unraveling the interconnections can help explain some of the nation's most troubling social problems and, more importantly, provide direction for their resolution (Holland 1986). To do so, however, first requires moving beyond the simplistic, individualistic, and moralistic explanations that have dominated much of the policymaking process and scholarly activity of recent years.

The intersection of restructuring, redevelopment, and race are increasingly manifested in everyday life, as will be illustrated throughout subsequent chapters. Globalization of the U.S. economy is characterized most explicitly by the loss of manufacturing jobs (1.9 million between 1979 and 1987, many of which were relocated to foreign shores) and the concentration of managerial and administrative functions at home contributing to a 13.9 million increase in service sector jobs. While this reflects some growth in highly paid professional positions, far more of the job creation is in unskilled, low-paid positions. Consequently, during the 1980s productivity grew 11.6 percent while hourly wages fell by 4.5 percent (Mishel and Simon 1988, 25; Mishel and Frankel 1990, 2). As part of this process of industrial restructuring, the built environment of cities changed. Downtown redevelopment was stimulated by the growth of financial and related producer services industries, suburbs continued to grow to house the professional employees of these firms and provide friendlier environments for diverse industries—including manufacturing, while formerly prosperous blue-collar industrial communities located between downtown and the suburbs deteriorated. Given their concentration in heavy industry and central city residential areas, racial minorities and particularly blacks have been adversely affected by these trends as evidenced by the fact that black family income as a percentage of white family income dropped from 60 percent in 1968 to 58 percent in 1991 nationwide after rising slowly but steadily for several decades. The decline was even steeper within large metropolitan areas—from 64 percent to 57 percent (U.S. Bureau of the Census 1969, 1992a, 1992b).

These structural developments are not, however, the natural outcome of market forces or an inevitable process of "creative destruction" in which higher uses of capital are pursued through entrepreneurial endeavors. They reflect politics broadly defined; that is, conflicting interests—primarily those associated with race and class—in which groups with varying power struggle to preserve their privileged position or achieve a more privileged position in American society. The critical distinctions are not those of government versus the private sector or central planning versus the market. In fact government policy and private sector activity through both planning and market forces have generally reflected those inequalities of race and class that have served as the principle dynamics shaping uneven development and social change in the United States.

The flight of manufacturing jobs from the United States to foreign shores, for example, as well as corporate relocations within the United States, downsizing (or "rightsizing") of industry, and other forms of economic restructuring all reflect the efforts of capital to seek out cheaper, union-free work forces in order to retain as large a share of surplus wealth as possible. Technological innovations in production and communication may facilitate these developments and make certain forms of restructuring feasible today that would have been impossible yesterday, but the underlying driving forces are social rather than technical (Harrison and Bluestone 1988; Bowles et al. 1983; Shaiken 1984). And the racial effects are not simply unintended outcomes of changes rooted elsewhere. When corporations seek out greener pastures they tend to seek out whiter ones as well, in part because of the presumption of a relatively greater attraction to unions on the part of blacks, in part to avoid equal opportunity requirements by avoiding areas where minorities are not in the picture, and in part due to the perpetuation of traditional stereotypes and old-fashioned prejudice (Cole and Deskins 1989; Stuart 1983; Kirschenman and Neckerman 1991).

These developments reflect public policy as well as private sector activity. As will be detailed in subsequent chapters, tax and regulatory policies have encouraged capital mobility, strengthened the hand of capital in labor-management struggles, and subsidized racial segregation and inequality. Particularly in the case of housing and housing finance, federal government policies and the policies and practices of private industry (most notably real estate, insurance, and mortgage lending) have been explicitly predicated on racial considerations with preservation of racially homogeneous neighborhoods a primary objective (Massey and Denton 1993; Jackson 1985; Tobin 1987). If these practices have been justified in terms of maintaining property values or neighborhood stability, they were based on racist assumptions and have had dramatically segregative and racist effects on urban development.

Given these institutional relationships and developments, a series of vicious circles are reinforced. Increasing economic competition from foreign trading partners and the U.S. political response to these developments have led to deindustrialization and disinvestment of cities. This process destroys the jobs base for many communities, reduces the revenues to support education and other essential public services, and increases the chasm between predominantly white suburbs and increasingly black inner cities. The deterioration of urban communities, of course, makes them less attractive to private investment, thus expediting their decline. Those who can, often escape, and those who cannot often resort to socially unacceptable survival strategies (e.g., crime, welfare dependency) or give up hope entirely and drift into drugs, homelessness, and self-destruction. It is not surprising that poverty grows and is increasingly concentrated in inner city neighborhoods, that racial tensions arise, and that "quiet riots" (e.g. poverty, unemployment, family disintegration, high crime rates, drug abuse, teenage pregnancy) along with not so quiet riots are occurring in cities around the nation (Harris and Wilkins 1988). Perhaps what is most perplexing is that, given these complex social realities, the predominant tendency in recent years has been to explain them away with simplistic, moralistic, and individualistic explanations and policy prescriptions.

Cultural Explanations for Structural Problems

As William J. Wilson (1987) cogently observed, when the passage of major civil rights legislation and enactment of Great Society social programs was followed a decade later by growing poverty and increasing racial inequality in urban America, an opportunity was created for conservative intellectuals and policymakers. If liberal social programs could not resolve these problems of the cities, perhaps conservatives were correct in asserting that government intervention, no matter how well-intentioned, generally only makes things worse (Friedman 1962). Liberal programs of the 1960s, of course, emphasized the centrality of racial discrimination and unequal opportunity, but their proponents—along with conservative critics—could not foresee the dramatic global and local structural changes that were emerging in the late 1960s and would hit with full force in the early 1970s. If traditional liberal and conservative policies were not effective in the face of these changes, conservatives struck first in attributing rising problems to the flaws they had always seen in liberal approaches.

The conservative assault on liberal social programs came from a diverse group of scholars, writers, and policymakers including George

Gilder, Charles Murray, Lawrence Mead, Richard Rodriguez, Linda Chavez, Thomas Sowell, Glen Loury, Shelby Steele, and many others. But they reflected and reinforced a common philosophy. Its basic contentions are the following: (1) the growing poverty, racial inequality, and "underclass" behavior that occurred in recent years reflect defects in the values and the culture of poor people themselves; (2) particularly problematic values include inadequate respect for the work ethic and a "live for today" mentality, with one key cultural manifestation being the breakup of the traditional family; (3) government programs unintentionally nurture a culture of dependency which perpetuates poverty and underclass behavior and; (4) only by forcing people to take care of themselves will these problems ever be effectively addressed.

In essence, a growing population of undeserving poor people— basically people who will not work—is concentrated in the nation's cities. As Lawrence Mead concluded, "In the absence of prohibitive barriers to employment, the question of the personality of the poor emerges as the key to understanding and overcoming poverty. . . . Experience has driven policymakers toward my own conclusion, that psychic inhibition, not a lack of opportunity, is the greatest impediment to employment" (Mead 1992, 133, 159). Even among those who do work, many are not successful, again, because of poor personal habits. As Thomas Sowell observed, "One of the most important causes of differences in income and employment is the way people work—some diligently, carefully, persistently, cooperatively, and without requiring much supervision or warnings about absenteeism, tardiness, or drinking, and others requiring much such concern over such matters" (Sowell 1984, 46–47). Acknowledging that some might dismiss observable group differences as evidence of bias or stereotyping, he concludes that "there is some evidence that cannot be disposed of in that way" (Sowell 1984, 47).

Much underclass behavior may well be the logical and predictable response to incentives that are inadvertently created by government, according to this perspective. Welfare programs—particularly AFDC—and civil rights agencies encourage some people to seek out various nonwork options; collecting welfare payments or pursuing civil rights complaints. And if these activities prove more rewarding than jobs that are available with a similar amount of effort, those are the options that a rational person would select (Murray 1984). In so doing, dependency is fostered while entrepreneurship and the associated attributes (aggressiveness, innovation, leadership) which are the keys to accumulating wealth are stifled (Gilder 1981).

All of these analysts acknowledge that discrimination has been an unfortunate part of the nation's history. But it is a far less significant factor today and, according to some, it has virtually disappeared. To

Sowell, "The battle for civil rights was fought and won—at great cost—many years ago" (Sowell 1984, 109). Shelby Steele notes that discrimination remains a fact of life. However, he concludes that what is holding blacks back is not discrimination but rather their own "victim-focused identity." That is, by investing so heavily in their status as victims and pursuing collective redress from white America, blacks are failing to take advantage of the opportunities that are available to them if they would just develop their individual abilities. To Steele, "the American black, supported by a massive body of law and the not inconsiderable goodwill of his fellow citizens, is basically as free as he or she wants to be" (Steele 1990, 175). But in order to take advantage of that freedom, "To retrieve our individuality and find opportunity, blacks today must—consciously or unconsciously—disregard the prevailing victim-focused identity . . . it curbs individualism and initiative, diminishes our sense of possibility, and contributes to our demoralization and inertia. . . . There will be no end to despair and no lasting solution to any of our problems until we rely on individual effort within the American mainstream—rather than collective action against the mainstream—as our means of advancement" (Steele 1990, 172–73). What may be even more problematic is that dependency is trickling down (or out) to other groups in "an orgy of competitive victimhood" (Mead 1992, 260). Echoing a now popular theme Mead concludes "claiming the status of victim leads only to dependency; it cannot promote social harmony or progressive change. For those goals, some greater self-reliance, a willingness to absorb injuries rather than flaunt them, is simply indispensable" (Mead 1992, 260).

If government has any role in this scenario, it is to nurture aggregate economic growth which will benefit all groups, though not necessarily or even preferably on an equal basis. Creation of wealth in the private sector, not government-mandated redistribution (whether through transfer payments, affirmative action programs, or other "artificial" means) is the key. If a community or region is declining while others are prospering, such uneven development simply reflects natural adjustments to technological change and market forces. Places as well as people may become redundant as the economic base of entire communities is shattered by national transformations (Anderson et al. 1983). The response should be to develop "pro people rather than pro place" policies and facilitate the relocation of families from areas that are shrinking to those that are growing (Peterson 1985; President's Commission for a National Agenda for the Eighties 1980). Government, in other words, is simply the junior partner whose job is to facilitate private capital accumulation.

Many acknowledge that education and training are key long-term needs and that government does have a role here. But the more important short-term and long-term objective is to eradicate dependency and, if necessary, force people to take care of themselves. As Mead claims, "There is a culture of poverty that discourages work, but the poor will work more regularly if government enforces the work norm" (Mead 1992, 24). Murray is even more direct when he advocates "scrapping the entire federal welfare and income-support structure for working-aged persons, including AFDC, Medicaid, Food Stamps, Unemployment Insurance, Worker's Compensation, subsidized housing, disability insurance, and the rest. It would leave the working-aged person with no recourse whatsoever except the job market, family members, friends, and public or private locally funded services. It is the Alexandrian solution: cut the knot, for there is no way to untie it" (Murray 1984, 227–28). And if public support of any kind is to be given, it must be tied to commitments for "responsible" behavior (e.g., school attendance, work) on the part of recipients. As New York journalist Jim Sleeper argued, "irresponsibility does not justify more irresponsibility . . . even one's status as a unique kind of social creditor does not exempt one from traditional social obligations" (Sleeper 1990, 311). If these proposals appear harsh, proponents claim it would be even crueler to perpetuate a culture of dependency which will only serve to entrap future generations in poverty.

Today, it is not just conservatives who demand such a quid pro quo from the poor. Bill Clinton's "A New Covenant for America's Cities" calls for welfare recipients to be required to take a job within two years of receiving benefits. "We will go nowhere unless individuals take responsibility for their own lives, working ceaselessly to overcome challenges and solve problems in their families and communities" (Clinton undated, 5–6). The conservative backlash to the liberal social programs of the 1960s may not be as influential in the 1990s as it was in the 1980s. But its penetration of traditionally liberal thought demonstrates that such thinking remains a strong force in scholarly and policymaking circles.

This approach to poverty, racial inequality, and economic development has been tried, and found wanting. As indicated above and as will be discussed in the following chapters, the anticipated economic growth did not occur, the buying power of the average income has declined, poverty has increased, racial inequalities in key economic areas have worsened, and the deterioration of cities continues. In one case study where conservative assumptions and policies prevailed—the city of Atlanta—Gary Orfield and Carole Ashkinaze (1991) found that racial barriers remained and in many areas were strengthened. They observe that in the late 1970s and 1980s Atlanta experienced economic growth, the city had a tight labor market, and blacks held key leadership positions. If the market policies proposed by the conservatives would ameliorate racial inequality, the authors argue, Atlanta should have proven the case. They observe, however, that segregation persisted particularly in housing which perpetuated unequal access to essential public and private benefits like good schools and jobs. In part because black elected leaders had to pursue conservative economic policies to retain businesses in the city, Orfield and Ashkinaze conclude they were limited in terms of what they could accomplish in the area of racial inequality, demonstrating once again the need for strong federal civil rights enforcement efforts.

The failure of the conservative policy initiatives was built in right from the start principally because of the blinders worn by the most influential proponents and the self-interest of the relatively few who in fact benefited. Ignorance (or avoidance) of the reality of class and racial conflict, unequal power relations, the exercise of that power to perpetuate privilege at one end and the lack of it at the other—in essence a failure to fully appreciate the reality of social structure—characterizes the conservative assault. What Benjamin DeMott (1990) has referred to as "the myth of classlessness"—the notion that virtually all Americans are part of one large middle class—obfuscates the reality of class, whitewashing unearned advantage and undercutting the implementation of truly progressive public policy in the process. The conservative perspective builds on this mythology by defining poverty and associated behaviors as characteristics of selected individuals rather than as structural dimensions of a social system. As Michael Katz observed, "poverty ... slipped easily, unreflectively, into a language of family, race, and culture rather than inequality, power, and exploitation" (Katz 1989, 8). Individual behavior and attitudes are important, of course, but they are only pieces of the broader sociological puzzle.

> By individualizing poverty, many American social scientists have aided the mystification of its origins and obscured its politics. ... For finally the politics of poverty are about the processes of inclusion and exclusion in American life: Who, to put the question crudely, gets what? How are goods distributed? As such, it is a question of race, class, gender, and the bases of power. Poverty is not an unfortunate accident, a residue, an indication that the great American mobility machine missed a minority of the people. On the contrary, always it has been a necessary result of America's distinctive political economy. (Katz 1989, 237)

The mystification is not simply the result of flawed analytical thinking. The major infusion of funding to support conservative intellectuals through think tanks and foundations like the American Enterprise Institute, the Hoover Institute, the Bradley Foundation, and many others demonstrates that these intellectual debates are part of a much broader set of conflicts within the American political economy. Self-interest is evident in how such scholarship is supported and disseminated. It should not be surprising that self-interest creeps into the core of the ideas themselves. By attributing primary causation of poverty and related problems to the characteristics of the individual victims themselves, a clear if unstated implication is that the nonpoor achieved their rank principally on the basis of their own individual effort. (Vernon Jordan, former Executive Director of the Urban League, related a revealing story from a conversation he had with a successful white businessman on a flight from New York to the West Coast. After his first martini the businessman observed that black people had to pull themselves up by their own bootstraps. After the third martini the businessman acknowledged that he went to an elite Eastern private college on the GI bill, started his business with a loan from the U.S. Small Business Administration, and purchased his Scarsdale home with an FHA loan. As Jordan concluded, "So much for lifting yourself up by your own bootstraps." Jordan 1991, 6.) If conventional notions about rugged individualism are misguided, such self-serving thought still provides a powerful rationalization for overall patterns of the distribution of income, wealth, and other valued goods. Equally important, the conservative vision reinforces the belief that little can be done, particularly by government, to remedy the situation. If government has served as a powerful force for creating and nurturing various forms of inequality in the past, the basic changes proposed for government today by conservative advocates—to reduce taxes, social spending, and regulation—coincidentally directly benefit the wealthy at the expense of the poor. Perhaps most importantly, to quote Katz once more, "They also conflict with the fewest vested interests because they do not require income redistribution or the sharing of power and other resources" (Katz 1989, 209).

Traditional American culture denies the existence of class, yet the evidence of class is ubiquitous (DeMott 1990). In fact, the reality of class in the United States is widely recognized and understood, even if it is not articulated in the popular press or casual conversation. How else can the popularity of the television show *Roseanne* or the appeal of the movie *Roger and Me* be explained? Or take the Northwestern University students who, while watching their Wildcats take another drubbing from the University of Illinois basketball team, chant in unison during the closing moments, "That's all right, that's OK, you're going to work for us someday."

The following chapters will illustrate how the conservative policy agenda reinforced various dimensions of inequality associated with global economic restructuring, the spatial development of cities, and race relations not just in Atlanta but urban America generally. If this cultural explanation and the ensuing policies failed to address these structural problems, this contradiction did not in fact begin with the resurgence of conservative thought in the 1970s and 1980s. The central themes of this perspective reflect a longstanding tradition of privatism that has shaped economic policy, urban redevelopment efforts, and responses to the social problems of U.S. cities.

Privatism and a Progressive Response

Throughout U.S. history there has been a longstanding, if sometimes uneasy, alliance between the public and private sectors. One shared understanding has dominated that relationship—the belief that government's job is to facilitate business development. Going back to the "public improvements" of the eighteenth and nineteenth centuries centering on the construction of waterways and railroads up through the twentieth century construction of highways and airports along with the enactment of tariffs, tax abatements, and other public aid, government has long subsidized the growth of private industry. The overriding justification for such public subsidies is captured by what has become known as the ideology of privatism (Warner 1987; Barnekov et al. 1989).

The ideology of privatism asserts that: (1) the driving force of productivity is the individual desire to improve one's material existence; (2) private enterprise and the free market are the most appropriate vehicles for nurturing that self-interest and assuring the most efficient production and distribution of goods and services; and (3) the role of government is to support those activities that will stimulate individual initiative and private capital accumulation.

Given these longstanding and deeply held assumptions regarding the linkage between individual self-interest and productivity, the efficiency of the market mechanism for regulating human activity and the allocation of resources, and the superiority of the private sector over government in encouraging wealth-producing activity, the rise of conservative thought in the last two decades reflects continuity with the past rather than a radical departure. From supply-side economics at the national level to "pro people" policy at the local level, it is evident that the dominance of privatism prevails. And as will be shown in subsequent chapters, the inequality that has characterized economic development, the spatial development of cities, and the social problems of urban America (particularly those associated with poverty and racial inequality) is directly linked to the assumptions and policies that have resulted from the commitment to privatism.

But that domination is not total. More democratic alternatives are being proposed, and in some cases implemented, to address the inter-related problems of economic productivity growth, urban development, and inequality. The next four chapters address specific critical policy issues: employment, housing, housing and community development finance, and urban redevelopment policy. In each case major theoretical and policy debates are examined and directions for future policy are indicated.

The following chapter on employment delineates the limitations of predominant individualistic (e.g., human capital) explanations for inequalities associated with employment and, in turn, income and wealth. Bringing in the structure of traditional workplace organizations provides a clearer understanding of such inequalities and suggests more democratic approaches to work that can yield greater productivity and more equitable outcomes. Employee ownership is examined to illustrate the potential of workplace democracy for ameliorating inequalities associated with class and race as well as for improving the productivity of individual firms and the economy generally.

The salience of race in the development of housing policy and, in turn, the role of housing policy in reinforcing racial inequalities are explored in chapter 3. The fallacies of privatistic assumptions about housing patterns as simply the outcome of individual buyers and sellers meeting in the marketplace are revealed and directions for more effective and more equitable housing policy are provided.

The examination of housing continues in chapter 4 which focuses on the central role of housing and community development finance in the uneven development of metropolitan areas. Debates over redlining and, again, the explicit use of race in determining property values and providing financial services are analyzed along with the diverse social costs of such practices for urban communities. Successful efforts to turn disinvestment into reinvestment, led primarily by community-based organizations, are reviewed along with the policy implications of these campaigns.

Chapter 5 examines urban redevelopment policy focusing on the emerging dominance of public-private partnerships as the critical tool. The influence of privatism—along with its limitations—are most vividly demonstrated in this area. At the same time, a variety of alternative approaches to redevelopment have been proposed and in some cases implemented in recent years which offer promise of more effective and equitable patterns of development.

In each of these chapters, the particular issue is examined within the context of the intersection of the structural, spatial, and social dimensions. And in each case directions for future policy and specific policy recommendations are offered, frequently based on current experiments and experiences. These efforts challenge the ideology of privatism, implicitly in most cases but explicitly in some, in attempts to pursue a more democratic approach and realize more progressive outcomes.

The final chapter delineates the critical elements and parameters that need to be reflected in any discussion of future policy if the limitations of the politics of privatism are to be overcome. Specifically, the values on which policy is premised, the arenas in which discussions and actions are carried out, and methods to be utilized to achieve more productive and equitable outcomes are examined from the perspective of a progressive rather than privatized city.

The national political climate of the 1990s is more conducive to an open debate over issues of racial inequality, urban blight, and the social costs of economic restructuring than was the case in the 1980s. Whether it was the explosion in Los Angeles, the growing number of working poor, the continuing deterioration of the competitive position of key sectors of the United States in the global economy, or a combination of forces, problems of racial unrest, inequality generally, and the productivity of the national economy are increasingly recognized as "front burner" issues that must be addressed directly and not simply as inevitable consequences of market forces to which the nation must acquiesce. If privatism remains a dominant ideological force, community organizations, political leaders at all levels, and many within the corporate sector recognize at least the possibility of strategic public and community-based intervention and planning to ameliorate these festering social problems.

Jimmy Carter's admonition regarding the duality of American cities sounds uncomfortably similar to the often quoted warning of the Kerner Commission in 1968, "To continue present policies is to make permanent the division of our country into two societies; one, largely Negro and poor, located in the central cities; the other, predominantly white and affluent, located in the suburbs and in outlying areas" (*Report of the National Advisory Commission on Civil Disorders* 1968, 22). Today, even many longtime civil rights advocates are questioning whether or not integration is a worthy goal to pursue.

The United States, of course, is increasingly fragmented along several dimensions. Racial conflicts go beyond blacks and whites involving as well Hispanics (Cubans, Mexicans, Puerto Ricans, and others), Asians (Chinese, Hmong, Japanese, Koreans, and others), and Native Americans. Conflicts among various ethnic and religious groups have increased in recent years. Gendered rules and relationships shape all vital social institutions and have influenced policy in virtually every area of public and private life. Regional battles between cities and suburbs, sunbelt and snowbelt states, and more recently between coastal communities and the central states have cropped up. The occupational structure is increasingly segmented and class distinctions have become crystallized (Fainstein et al. 1992; Mollenkopf and Castells 1991; Smith and Feagin 1987; Sassen 1988, 1992).

But the predominant trajectories of uneven development remain restructuring and globalization of the national economy, the spatial development of metropolitan areas, and the growing inequality of income and wealth among local citizens. If cities are increasingly multicultural, race remains the most divisive split and black/white conflicts remain the most salient (Galster and Hill 1992; Massey and Denton 1993). The duality noted from the Kerner Commission in 1968 to Jimmy Carter in 1992 still captures the fundamental dynamic of urban life.

Theories and policies grounded in the personality, culture, or other sets of characteristics about individuals cannot help but fail to explain the serious social problems plaguing American cities. In order to illuminate what are fundamentally social phenomena, the focus of attention must be the central structural characteristics and patterns of segmentation occurring in American society. In turn policy must focus on the fault lines of segmentation constituted by economic restructuring, spatial development, and racial conflict if the social costs of these developments are to be ameliorated.

2

Deindustrialization, Economic Democracy, and Equal Employment Opportunity: The Changing Context of Race Relations in Urban America

We believe policies that do not take into account the changing characteristics of the national economy—including its rate of growth and demand for labor, including factors that affect industrial employment such as investment and technology, and including demographic changes that accompany industrial transformations—cannot possibly respond effectively to the economic and social dislocations of low-income blacks.

Joint Center for Political Studies, 1983

In its annual report, *The State of Black America 1988,* the National Urban League concluded that "more blacks have lost jobs through industrial decline than through job discrimination" (Dewart 1988, 155). Hardly insensitive to the realities of racism, the Urban League is attuned to the increasingly complex dynamics that shape the objective conditions of black life, particularly at the core of urban America today.

The persistence of racial disparities in many critical socioeconomic indicators over the past two decades suggests that racism may indeed be as American as apple pie. Yet there have been many legal victories in the civil rights arena, the number of black elected officials has multiplied and available evidence suggests increasing acceptance of equal opportunity among all groups in American society. At the same time, there have been dramatic changes in the structure of the U.S. economy and its labor market that have adversely affected both U.S. cities and the nation's minority population. If many of these changes have been inextricably connected with evolving patterns of race relations in America, it is also true that many of the forces shaping urban communities, and adversely affecting minorities, cannot be explained primarily in terms of race.

There has been much debate in recent years over the relative significance of race and class in determining the objective life-chances of minorities (Wilson 1978, 1987; Willie 1979; Landry 1987; Jencks and Peterson 1991; Jencks 1992; Feagin 1991; Marable 1991). Most partisans to this debate have contributed to a fuller understanding of the changing realities of urban communities and the nation as a whole. Unfortunately, the debate has occasionally been polarized into unproductive, either/or terms. That important racial disparities persist in American life is simply a matter of documented fact. Equally true is the continuing reality of racial prejudice. The context of race relations, however, has changed in the past twenty years.

Central to understanding the frustration encountered by policymakers trying to reduce racial inequality are the ideological blinders that shape most analyses of race relations and urban development. Such work has been rooted in an individualistic framework, consistent with the ideology of privatism, that is most explicit in human capital theories of racial inequality. Emerging neoconservative analyses of the so-called underclass, the nature of urban poverty, and the role of race, build upon the individualistic assumptions that have long informed the neoclassical tradition in general, particularly its human-capital proponents (Gilder 1981; Murray 1984; Mead 1992). Ignored by this perspective are the structural determinants of racial inequality and uneven development, determinants that have assumed increasing importance in the postwar globalization of the U.S. economy. As indicated in the previous chapter, the disjunction between structural causes and individualistic explanations of uneven development and racial inequality gave rise to growing disenchantment with the potential of liberal reforms and opened the door to neoconservative contentions that little could be done in the policy arena, particularly in terms of government intervention, to mitigate these problems (Wilson 1987).

To effectively address the seemingly immutable facts of racial inequality and uneven urban development, structural responses to structural problems are needed. These include macroeconomic problems now reaching global dimensions as well as microeconomic issues including the internal structure of individual firms and other organizations that provide employment. The phenomenon of employee ownership, particularly in its more democratic formulations, illustrates how structural economic change can give rise to greater racial equality and ameliorate uneven development, as will be demonstrated below.

Deindustrialization of the nation's urban core and the flight of capital to the suburbs, the sunbelt and beyond are the central structural forces that have devastated many urban communities and contributed directly to the persistence of racial inequality in those communities. Such unchecked, uncontrolled, and uneven development can be addressed through more democratic intervention into what have traditionally been viewed as the prerogatives of the ownership and management of private businesses. More democratic economic structures in general, particularly many of the organizational characteristics frequently associated with employee ownership, offer potentially powerful tools for addressing the changing dynamics of race relations in urban America. None of this suggests any curtailment in equal employment opportunity law enforcement, voluntary affirmative action programs, or other civil rights initiatives, or diminishes the need for more effective macroeconomic policies and local redevelopment initiatives. For an urban policy to effectively address the issue of racial inequality, though, it must complement traditional, liberal civil rights remedies with other tactics that will inject a strong dose of democracy into the nation's economic institutions. This chapter examines the changing context of race relations over the past two decades and explores critical policy implications.

The Continuing Significance of Race

Employment and income may be the two most critical indicators of objective life conditions and relative status of individuals and groups in American society. According to these two indicators, racial disparities in the nation and its cities have remained the same or increased since the landmark Kerner Commission report warned that the United States was on the verge of dividing into two societies (*Report of the National Advisory Commission on Civil Disorder* 1968). Officially, nonwhite unemployment in 1968 was 6.7 percent nationwide, compared to 3.2 percent for whites, a nonwhite/white ratio of 2.2. In 1991, nonwhite unemployment rose to 11.1 percent and white unemployment reached 6 percent for a ratio of 1.9. Within the nation's metropolitan areas, however, the nonwhite/white unemployment ratio rose from 1.9 percent in 1973 to 2.1 percent in 1991. Labor-force participation rates reflect similar racial disparities. The nonwhite, nationwide labor-force participation rate (62.2 percent) was actually higher than the white rate (59.3 percent) in 1973. By 1990 the nonwhite labor force participation rate (63.1 percent) was less than the white rate (66.6 percent). In the nation's central cities, whites had a slight advantage over nonwhites in 1973 (60.3 percent vs. 59.9 percent), which increased by 1990 to 66.0 percent versus 61.2 percent (Hamal 1988; U.S. Department of Labor 1991).

Family income figures in the United States reveal a similar story. As indicated in the previous chapter, median black family income as a percentage of median white family income dropped form 60.0 percent in 1968 to 57.1 percent in 1991 (U.S. Bureau of the Census 1987a, b, 1992a); in metropolitan areas the decline was from 63.7 percent to 57.1 percent, while for metropolitan areas with a population more than one million, the decline among central-city families was steeper, from 69.7 percent to 57.3 percent (U.S. Bureau of the Census 1969, 1987b, 1992b).

During these years poverty increased, but the black/white poverty ratio declined from 3.4 to 3.0. Within metropolitan areas, however, the poverty rate increased for both groups while the black/white ratio remained constant at 2.4 within central cities, but declined from 4.3 to 2.9 in the suburbs (U.S. Bureau of the Census 1971, 1992c).

These disparities persisted despite several positive developments in civil rights and race relations. Federal civil rights laws have been strengthened and the number of equal opportunity laws and programs at the state and local levels has grown. Despite efforts by the Reagan administration to turn back the clock on civil rights (Chambers 1987), the U.S. Supreme Court issued several decisions in 1986 and 1987 that rejected Reagan's interpretation of federal equal employment opportunity laws and advanced affirmative action efforts. Contrary to the Reagan administration's claim that Title VII of the Civil Rights Act of 1964 (the principal federal statute outlawing employment discrimination) applies only to individual, identifiable victims of discrimination and allows only for "make-whole" relief for actual victims of an employer's illegal discrimination, the Supreme Court has interpreted that act much more broadly. In *Wygant v. Jackson Board of Education,* the Court ruled that governments may be allowed to use hiring preferences for minorities to redress past discriminations. In *Firefighters v. City of Cleveland,* the Court found constitutional a plan to hire one black or Hispanic for each white person hired, claiming that voluntary plans "may include reasonable race-conscious relief that benefits individuals who were not actual victims of discrimination." In *Local 28 Sheetmetal Workers v. EEOC* the Court upheld a 29-percent hiring quota arguing, in part, that "the purpose of affirmative action is not to make identified victims whole, but rather to dismantle prior patterns of employment discrimination." In *Johnson v. Santa Clara County Transportation Agency,* the Court confirmed that race or sex could be taken into consideration in hiring or promotion decisions even in the absence of a prior finding of discrimination on the part of the employer.

In a series of decisions handed down in 1989 (*Richmond v. Croson, Wards Cove Packing Co. v. Atonio, Martin v. Wilks, Lorance v. AT&T, Patterson v. McLean Credit Union,* and *Jett v. Dallas Independent School District*), the Court placed additional burdens on minority plaintiffs' and others' efforts to enforce federal nondiscrimination rules and implement affirmative action plans. In response, Congress enacted and, after almost two years of debate, President Bush signed, the Civil Rights Act of 1991 which removed those impediments (Leadership Conference Education Fund 1992).

In addition to these legal victories, black political participation has grown substantially in the past two decades. Prior to passage of the Voting Rights Act in 1965 there were fewer than 200 black elected officials in the United States. In 1992 there were approximately 8,000 (Persons 1987, 167; Ruffin 1993).

White Americans appear to have more tolerant attitudes toward blacks on most issues, particularly on the question of equal employment opportunity. If discrimination was taken for granted by white Americans as recently as the 1940s, the dominant expressed belief today is that blacks deserve equal treatment (Schuman, Steeh, and Bobo 1985; Firebaugh and Davis 1988).

The racial gap appears to be closing in other, more concrete, ways. Educational attainment differences are smaller today that just a few years ago. Among those working full time, and particularly younger college-educated workers, the occupational status and individual wages of blacks continued to move closer to that of whites in the 1980s (Farley 1984; O'Hare et al. 1991).

Despite areas in which gains have been made, disparities persist in most critical areas. As indicated above, the proportion of blacks and whites working full time remains as far apart today as it was twenty-five years ago. For most individuals, family income determines their objective life conditions, and the gap between blacks and whites in this area has increased. If there have been important legal, political and attitudinal advances, critical economic disparities remain.

The perpetuation of these racial disparities reflects, in part, fundamental structural changes in the American economy that evolved primarily in response to considerations other than race. The declining position of the United States in the international economy (the U.S. share of world economic output declined from 35 percent in 1960 to 22 percent in 1980 [Reich 1987, 44]), and the declining rate of profit in the post–World War II years, stimulated several responses on the part of corporate America to reverse the decline. A central objective of that strategy has been to solidify managerial control over production and surplus wealth generated by the economy. Technological advances in communication, transportation and production enabled U.S. manufacturers to expand their operations overseas, particularly in low-wage countries, and facilitated their efforts to shift investment and production around the globe. A range of antilabor tactics at home have been employed, and corporations have been able to pit capital-starved communities against each other in efforts to secure the most favorable terms of operation, from the corporate perspective (Bluestone and Harrison 1982, 1988; Bowles, Gordon, and Weisskopf 1983, 1990; Shaiken 1984—These issues are discussed in greater detail in subsequent chapters, particularly chapter 5).

Encouraged by supply-side tax cuts and an antiregulation climate at the federal level, corporate America demanded and received further incentives from state and local governments (e.g., tax abatements, industrial revenue bonds, land cost write-downs) which felt the only available response was to "meet the competition" (Goodman 1979). In the 1980s, urban policy virtually disappeared in the name of "reindustrialization." *Business Week* (1980) argued that the "aspirations of the poor, the minorities, [and other] special-interest groups must recognize that their own unique goals cannot be satisfied if the U.S. cannot compete in world markets." President Carter's Commission for a National Agenda for the Eighties, in prescient anticipation of his successor, argued that the "economic health of our nation's communities ultimately depends on the health of our nation's economy," which in turn depends on the creation of "an attractive investment climate." Claiming that "cities are not permanent," the commission argued, in the spirit of Joseph Schumpeter's concept of "creative destruction," that federal policy should be directed toward moving people to where the jobs are and to letting cities go through their natural "transformation" (President's Commission for a National Agenda for the Eighties 1980, 64–72, 165–69). Recently there has been more expressed concern for the plight of cities. It remains to be seen how effectively the stated concerns will be translated into policy.

This definition of the situation expedited the flight of capital from the United States to foreign shores. Urban to suburban shifts were well documented in the 1960s, triggering the previously noted observation of the Kerner Commission report. Unclear at that time was that these shifts constituted just part of a much larger pattern of uneven development, and that impending economic crisis would exacerbate such uneven development, with racial minorities again enduring a disproportionate share of the burden.

Racial minorities are concentrated precisely in those geographic locations, industries, and occupations that have been hardest hit by deindustrialization. Almost 58 percent of all blacks live in central cities, compared to just 26 percent of whites (O'Hare et al. 1991, 9). While minorities constitute approximately 12 percent of the U.S. work force, they represent more than 14 percent of auto and steel workers, two of the hardest hit industries. Managerial and professional positions, in which unemployment rates have generally remained below 5 percent even when total unemployment reached double digits, appear to be better protected from the vicissitudes of uneven development. Blacks, though, are half as likely as whites to be employed in these occupational classifications (Hearings before the Subcommittee on Economic Stabilization 1984, 43). Mismatches noted by Kain (1968) twenty-five years ago, between the skills possessed by minorities and available jobs, have been exacerbated by contraction of manufacturing jobs and expansion of financial, administrative, and related professional service jobs in the nation's cities in recent years. Among displaced workers, blacks are unemployed for longer periods of time and when these workers do find jobs, blacks earn a lower percentage of their previous wages than do whites (Lichter 1988; Moore 1992).

Capital mobility adversely affects minorities in many additional ways. Holding a disproportionately small share of equity in American businesses, minorities receive a disproportionately small share of profits from plant closings, openings, and relocations. (The typical white household has twelve times the net worth and almost four times the equity in a business or profession of the typical black household [Tidwell 1987, 195, 202]). Particularly when a plant moves from a central city to a suburban location, minorities face greater difficulties in finding transportation to the jobs or housing in the new location. Consequently, minorities are more likely not to move with the firm (assuming they have that option) or to quit after a short time because of the logistical problems created by the move. When new jobs are created in the suburbs, minorities are less likely to hear about, and therefore apply for, those positions. In many ways, some of which have little if anything to do with an explicit consideration of race, uneven development has adversely effected racial minorities in the United States (Illinois Advisory Committee 1981; Galster and Hill 1992; Goldsmith and Blakely 1992).

In recent years, several economists and public officials have called for industrial policies that expressly acknowledge the conflicts that give rise to, and the social costs (including urban disinvestment and exacerbation of racial inequalities) that result from, capital mobility and uneven development. Specific ingredients of such proposals often include more effective targeting of resources to distressed areas, linkage requirements or performance standards to be met in exchange for public subsidies (including affirmative action and contract compliance requirements), plant-closing prenotification, and other tactics to protect public needs while serving private interests. A central focus of these proposals is the incorporation of workers, residents, and other members of the community who are affected by investment decisions into those decision-making processes that have traditionally been the sole prerogative of private capital. Recognizing the growing public costs of private enterprise, at least some observers have rejected supply-side incentives predicated on trickle-down assumptions in favor of a bargained or linkage approach to economic development and urban redevelopment, based on a more democratic approach to economic decisionmaking that seeks balanced growth as a direct outcome (Bluestone and Harrison 1982, 1988; Bowles, Gordon, and Weisskopf 1983, 1990; City of Chicago 1984; Mier, Moe, and Sherr 1986; Thurow 1981; Squires et al. 1987; Dreier and Ehrlich 1991; Keating 1986).

A central component of many such plans is advocacy (frequently coupled with commitment of financial and other concrete resources) for the creation of new business organizations, or restructuring of existing firms, to permit employees to participate in investment, production, and other management decisionmaking and, in turn, allow employees to share equitably in the rewards as well as the responsibilities of managing the business. Workplace democracy, as illustrated by employee ownership particularly in its more democratic configurations, embodies critical civil rights implications that have long been ignored.

Employee Ownership:
An Emerging Economic Phenomenon

Employee ownership has become an increasingly popular tool for economic development in recent years. Though the concept is certainly not without its critics, many benefits are attributed to employee ownership. Virtually no systematic attention has been paid, however, to the experiences of racial minorities in employee-owned firms or the civil rights implications of this type of business organization. There are, however, theoretically plausible reasons and scattered empirical evidence to suggest that employee ownership ameliorates employment disparities associated with race. An employee-owned Washington, D.C. insurance company, for example, paid its black employees an average salary of $21,200, compared to $30,100 for whites, a black/white ratio of .71 in 1984 (Mariam 1985). For the insurance industry as a whole in Washington, D.C., however, the black/white ratio was just .54 (U.S. Bureau of the Census 1981). Racial minorities clearly are doing far better relative to whites in this employee-owned company than they are industrywide in the nation's capital. There is reason to believe this racial effect is not unique to one employer.

A perusal of the popular press, academic journals, and the behavior of government agencies and other community organizations reveals a striking increase in the interest being paid to the concept and practice of employee ownership. Though not a new concept, the nation's recent economic troubles have led many observers to conclude that the time for employee ownership has come. Rosen, Klein, and Young (1986) of the National Center for Employee Ownership conclude that this form of ownership provides the solution for what are often viewed as contradictory ends: equity and growth. In their introduction, entitled "Mr. Smith, Meet Mr. Marx," they argue, "By making employees owners, programs that enhance capital investment automatically enrich workers" (1986, 5).

The idea of employee ownership in the United States is as old as the nation itself. The Founding Fathers frequently noted the utility of widespread property ownership, including business ownership, primarily as a device to assure the commitment of as many citizens as possible to the value of private property (Russell 1985, 8–11). Today it is an idea that appeals to all ends of the political spectrum, from Ronald Reagan, Russell Long, and the Pope to Ted Kennedy, Tom Hayden, and the Teamsters. Similarly, it is criticized by proponents of diverse political perspectives, including many representatives of the business community and organized labor. Today, though, there are more than 11,000 firms—representing more than 12 million workers, about 12 percent of the work force—in which employees share in the ownership. In most cases employees own between 15 and 40 percent, with employees owning a majority of stock in 10 to 15 percent (Blasi 1988; Rosen and Young 1991, 1–19; Rosen, Klein, and Young 1986, 1, 2, 16; Rosen and Quarry 1987). In recent years there has been increasing debate over the concept of employee ownership, along with more substantial public and private support of efforts to encourage the practice.

The motivations for turning employees into owners are diverse. A major attraction is the utility of employee ownership in raising capital for reinvestment (including leveraged buyouts to prevent hostile takeovers) or to facilitate the acquisition or divestiture of subsidiaries. This is particularly true for employee stock-ownership plans (ESOPs), which have grown from approximately 300 in 1974 to more than 7,000 today because of various federal tax breaks associated with this financing vehicle (Rosen, Klein, and Young 1986, 14–31; Russell 1985, 196–219). Another incentive is provided by evidence that employee-owned firms, compared to conventionally structured firms, are often more productive and more profitable, with one of the reasons for such performance being better labor relations and employee morale in such settings (Frieden 1980; Conte and Tannenbaum 1980; Blumberg 1973; Select Committee on Small Business 1979). Recent evidence also suggests that employee-owned firms grow more rapidly, in terms of sales and total employment, and such effects are greater where ownership and meaningful participation are combined (Rosen and Quarry 1987).

A related motivation is the desire to save a business through conversion to employee ownership that might otherwise be shut down (Midwest Center for Labor Research 1985; Rosen, Klein, and Young 1986, 27–29; Russell 1985, 193–219). Such initiatives can help strengthen ties between workers and their local community, enhance labor solidarity, and save many jobs in the process (Swinney 1985). As indicated above, the stagnation of the U.S. economy in recent years has convinced many within business, labor, and government to view employee ownership as part of the solution to economic ills in general, and to act on that belief (Russell 1985, 196–212). Many industrial policy and urban redevelopment proposals have incorporated elements of employee ownership (Bradley and Gelb 1983; Bluestone and Harrison 1982, 257–62; Bowles, Gordon, and Weisskopf 1983, 261–390). For some, the desire for a more democratic workplace provides a major attraction to employee ownership, particularly when coupled with worker control. In some instances, the more democratic structure is viewed as a means to more productive ends, while for others the appeal is for democracy as a value itself, regardless of any effect on productivity (Zwerdling 1978; Cohen and Rogers 1983).

At the same time, strong objections to employee ownership have been raised. In addition to the philosophy of some business leaders that "management's job is to manage," there are many within the labor movement who view employee ownership as antithetical to the interests of the majority of workers.

At a time when more militant tactics are required to confront capital, according to some (Slott 1985; Zwerdling 1978, 165–80), employee ownership results in complicity with management by labor leaders and redirection of union members' energy to helping their employers survive in the marketplace. Critics contend that cooperation with management pits workers against each other as they become unwitting collaborators with management. As workers identify with their own bosses rather than each other, it is feared they will acquiesce to speed ups and sacrifice even more control to management (Bluestone and Bluestone 1992, 168). A related contention is that employee ownership is simply the successor to bureaucratic control (Edwards 1979) as a mechanism for management to assure the loyalty of, and manipulate and control, their workers (Russell 1985, 197–202). Without additional structural changes that provide for control as well as ownership, an employee-owned firm, particularly in the form of an ESOP, may constitute "second-class ownership" for the workers, without any of the advantages traditionally associated with ownership (Ellerman 1985; Blasi 1988).

More concrete costs have been asserted. Employee ownership can be used as a vehicle for securing substantial wage cuts (Rothschild-Witt 1985; Lynd 1985). In some cases, workers assume extreme risks when their jobs, investments, and retirement funds become dependent on the profitability of one business, particularly if it is a financially troubled firm to begin with (Russell 1985, 205–7).

Despite these criticisms, employee ownership has grown, in no small part as a result of public support for turning employees into owners. Since 1973, there have been at least fifteen federal laws, along with legislation in more than fourteen states, to provide such aid as technical assistance in conducting feasibility studies, loans, tax breaks and other financial support for the creation of employee-owned businesses (Rosen, Klein, and Young 1986, 251–55).

Amid this flurry of activity, no attention has been paid to the civil rights implications of employee ownership. It has been argued that self-management can provide an effective structure for black economic development (Williams 1976) and that ESOPs constitute an effective vehicle for black capital accumulation (Whittaker 1977). No effort has been made, however, to systematically assess the effect of employee ownership on racial inequality, yet there are plausible arguments and scattered empirical evidence to suggest that at least some forms of employee ownership ameliorate racial disparities in the labor market.

Theoretical Perspectives on Racial Income Inequality

The potential of employee ownership as part of an urban policy geared toward the amelioration of racial inequality is demonstrated by recent theoretical developments in social science analyses of race relations. For any policy to be effective it must be premised on a sound theoretical understanding of the issue at hand. Important progress toward this end has been made in the area of race relations in recent years.

Human capital theory and the neoclassical paradigm in which it is rooted have long been the dominant conceptual tools used to explain the distribution of wages as well as inequalities associated with race. This perspective, as Donald Schwab told the U.S. Commission on Civil Rights, "has remained the principal economic explanation of micro wage-setting behavior for over 100 years" (U.S. Commission on Civil Rights 1985, 26). According to this perspective, wages and salaries are determined primarily by the demand for and supply of particular skills and services in a free, unitary labor market. Individual buyers (i.e., employers) and sellers (i.e., employees) meet in the marketplace to negotiate the price at which people will go to work, that is, the wage level at which the market will clear. The more skills, education, and experience desired by employers that an employee can bring to the market—the greater his or her human capital—the higher the price will be that the employer will have to pay for that employee. A free labor market, like the free market for any product or service, provides for maximum societal efficiency in the utilization of labor resources. In general, whites have accumulated more human capital than non-whites. Consequently, whites have been able to command higher wages (Friedman 1984).

While whites as a group possess more human capital, on average, than nonwhites, a central assumption of human capital theory and the neoclassical paradigm is that levels of education, experience, and career trajectory are functions of individual choice. A key question that each person confronts is whether to maximize current consumption (to be achieved in part by getting a job now) or to spend current time obtaining more education and training to maximize future consumption. Such preparation enhances future earnings because the individual would be qualified at a later time for jobs requiring higher levels of skill (and consequently paying higher wages) and the individual would be able to compete for a broader range of jobs, thus enhancing his or her opportunities to secure better-paying positions. The critical assumption, again, is that the job one holds or the career one chooses to pursue is the result of voluntary, individual choice, presumably unaffected by race, sex or any other social or cultural factors.

By explaining labor market and related economic inequalities among racial groups in these voluntaristic and individualistic terms, human capital theory provides a relatively simple and seemingly plausible solution to racial inequality that benefits not only those at the lower end of the economic spectrum, but the entire community. The basic solution resides in increased education and training. Not only will the individuals receiving these services benefit by accumulating more human capital and becoming more competitive in the labor market, society will benefit as well by the increasing productivity that results from a more highly skilled work force. To the extent that lower-income people obtain their fair share of education and training opportunities, economic equality will be enhanced, again because of market forces that operate in an open, competitive economy. As Lester Thurow (1972) has noted, there are three basic reasons, according to the human-capital perspective, why this is the case. First, increased education and training will help poor (and previously untrained) people obtain better jobs. Second, as the supply of unskilled workers diminishes, the growing scarcity of such workers will bid up the price of unskilled labor. Third, as the supply of highly skilled people increases, particularly where it exceeds demand, the price for such labor will decline.

Any discrepancies between the wages of whites and nonwhites that are not predicated on different levels of human capital cannot long prevail, according to the assumptions of the neoclassical paradigm. If a given employer were to pay whites higher wages than nonwhites who possess equivalent human capital, the workings of the free market will soon punish that employer. By exercising his or her taste for discrimination, that employer will be paying a higher wage for a given level of human capital than will the competition, ultimately forcing that employer out of business. The basic solutions to problems of discrimination, therefore, are the preservation of a free labor market (Becker 1957, 1964; Friedman 1962; Sowell 1981, 1984; Williams 1982).

This perspective has been challenged in recent years by many who reject the neoclassical paradigm and the ideology of privatism in general along with human-capital theory in particular. The fundamental points of contention are the assumption of a unitary labor market, reliance on characteristics of individuals to explain wage patterns and the voluntary nature in which career choices are presumably made. While not denying that positive returns are associated with education, skills, and related attributes, the dominant perspective ignores a range of structural characteristics of the economy and society generally that shape the overall distribution of wages as well as those associated with race. In efforts to overcome these deficiencies, alternative models have been offered.

Several economists and sociologists have advanced a number of dual-economy and segmentation conceptualizations. The dual economy, constituted by core and periphery firms (Averitt 1968; Tolbert, Horan, and Beck 1980) and a dual labor market consisting of primary- and secondary-sector jobs (Baron and Hymer 1971; Gordon, Edwards, and Reich 1982; Edwards, Reich, and Gordon 1975) have been identified in which wages are shaped by the characteristics of the sector, industry, and job of the individual, independent of the human capital he or she has accumulated. Such factors as industry and company size, concentration (monopoly vs. competitive), capital intensity, unionization rates and degree of government regulation define various sectors of the economy and influence wages paid within them. Wages are also frequently a function of the characteristics of jobs as well as of job holders. Primary sector jobs have been identified that are characterized by job security, opportunities for promotion, good working conditions, fair administration of work rules and higher earnings. Secondary jobs, on the other hand, offer little security, little chance for promotion, poor working conditions, arbitrary administration of work rules and promotion, and low earnings. Not only are human-capital theory's individualistic assumptions challenged by such segmentation, but to the extent that these sectors operate independently of each other (that is, workers compete within industrial sectors or job markets) unitary assumptions about the job market are undermined as well. Racial minorities are "crowded" (Bergmann 1971) into the less desirable jobs in such "split-labor markets" (Bonacich 1972), thus reducing their wages relative to whites and seriously challenging voluntary assumptions about career choice. Given these conditions, race ceases being just an individual characteristic, since wages are downgraded in those positions because they have a high concentration of racial minorities (Friedman 1984; U.S. Commission on Civil Rights 1985, 18).

Human-capital theory's reliance on the external labor market as the major wage setting force is challenged by researchers who have demonstrated that characteristics of internal labor markets frequently shape wage levels (Doeringer and Piore 1971). In efforts to reduce recruitment and training costs, and to stabilize the work force and reduce production costs generally, employers often offer higher wages and other benefits to current employees than they could receive in the external labor market. For example, an employer may rely on word-of-mouth advertising to fill new jobs, thus enabling employees to help their family and friends and reducing their own recruitment costs. When the current work force is predominantly white, one likely, though perhaps unintentional, result is to perpetuate the racial composition of the work force.

Employers may also seek a homogeneous work force in order to assure stable working relations and compatibility between employers and customers. If productivity is perceived not simply as an individual characteristic but rather as a feature of the social relations of work (among employees and between employees and customers), then discrimination may well be rational from the employers' perspective (Kirschenman and Neckerman 1991).

Other structural characteristics of organizations that deny opportunities to racial minorities have also been identified. Rigid hierarchical bureaucracies in which decisionmaking is highly centralized, narrowly defined job responsibilities that stifle human capital development, and a corporate culture that reinforces conformity to conventional stereotypes tend to restrict the opportunity, power, and informal support for employees at the lower rungs, particularly for racial minorities (Kanter 1977).

A variety of personnel practices shape the distribution of wages independently of the human capital of workers, mitigate the free play of the market, and adversely affect nonwhites. These include screening devices that use averages among diverse groups to draw conclusions about individual members that, intentionally or unintentionally, adversely affect racial minorities. Educational credentials unrelated to job requirements are often used as a convenience to the employer and to reduce recruiting costs, but at the expense of black applicants. Such "statistical discrimination" (Arrow 1972) has been declared illegal under certain circumstances, but this has not eliminated these practices nor ended their impact on racial inequality (U.S. Commission on Civil Rights 1981).

But sometimes statistical discrimination is clearly not devoid of racial intent. Often such practices are predicated on stereotypical notions employers still hold about black workers, particularly those who live in inner city neighborhoods. In one survey of Chicago area employers respondents spoke openly of the problematic work ethic of blacks compared with whites and Hispanics. Attributes that were said to characterize inner city workers included illiteracy, dishonesty, lack of motivation and initiative, instability, and other behaviors reflecting what many have referred to as the underclass (Kirschenman and Neckerman 1991). Given these perceptions, it is not surprising that researchers with the Urban Institute found that when identically matched pairs of black and white job seekers applied for the same entry level positions in Chicago and Washington D.C., a clear pattern of discrimination was found. In 20 percent of the cases the white applicant got further in the application process than the black candidate. The reverse was found in 7 percent. And in 15 percent of the cases the white applicant was offered the job when the black applicant was not. In 5 percent the black, but not the white, applicant received a job offer (Turner and Fix 1991).

Another factor that mitigates the operation of a truly free labor market is the unequal availability of information about job opportunities. A critical assumption of the neoclassical theory of free markets is universal availability of information among buyers and sellers. The absence of such universality means that those with information that others lack have an advantage, which undermines the operation of a free market. A free labor market would require that all participants be aware of all employment opportunities, and therefore be able to compete on the basis of the marginal productivities they bring to the market. Knowledge of job openings, though, is not universally available. Those who are part of, or have access to, the "right" networks have an obvious advantage. Where informal or subjective criteria are used in employment decisions, knowledge of opportunities may be limited strictly to those on the inside. Nonwhites are less likely to be part of such networks, particularly those involving the allocation of more prestigious and higher-paid positions.

Inequality in the training and education that people receive and in the economic resources held by themselves or their families prior to entering the labor market further undermines human-capital theory assumptions regarding the individual and voluntary nature of job and career choices. Unequal resources devoted to the education of whites and nonwhites, and racial steering by teachers, guidance counselors, and other school administrators, as well as other discriminatory practices within the nation's educational institutions, result in greater opportunity for whites to exercise free choice as they prepare for and enter their chosen careers. Since white families on average have more economic resources than nonwhites, white children are also more free to decide whether they want to take a job now and maximize current consumption or delay entry into the job market by getting more education, thereby maximizing future consumption. Obviously, when a family is poor and cannot afford either the cost of higher education or the foregone income resulting from fulltime school attendance, the voluntary nature of such choices is restricted (Rist 1970; Rehberg and Hotchkiss 1972; Carnoy and Levin 1985).

More radical formulations have focused on the failure of the neoclassical paradigm to account for the significance of class, conflict, and power relations in shaping wage levels. Human-capital theory has been effectively criticized for treating economic behavior as if it occurs independently of politics and other social relations and institutions (Friedman 1984). It is the unequal relation between capital and labor, however, that most fundamentally determines aggregate wage levels and the distribution among diverse populations (Reich 1981; Boggs and Boggs 1970; Geschwender 1977; Lieberson 1980).

The concept of a reserve army of labor, in which a steady pool of unemployed people provides employers with substantial leverage in negotiating wages along with other terms of employment, perhaps most explicitly illustrates this relationship. From this perspective, even if job training, information networks, and other supply-side factors were equalized, the lack of jobs would clearly constitute a major barrier to employment and equal opportunity. Recent studies have in fact confirmed that in major urban labor markets there are anywhere from seven to twelve job seekers for every available job (Abraham 1983; Lafer 1992; Wilburg and Wojno 1992). Given the competition and traditional "last hired first fired" practices, racial disparities are manifested that cannot be accounted for by the human capital possessed by job seekers. Such racial stratification and one's position in the class structure, as determined by the extent of control over the production process, consequently affect wages, independent of human capital considerations (Wright 1979). The reemergence of the phrase "political economy" symbolizes the thrust of this perspective.

Evidence of the political dimensions of wage allocations and other personnel practices includes the fact that such decisions are often shaped by the desire of capital to control labor, rationalize the production process, and preserve their privileged position in American society as well as by supply-and-demand conditions in the external labor market (Braverman 1974; Edwards 1979; Bowles et al. 1983, 1990). The ability of labor to resist such initiatives and to secure higher wages is, at least in part, a function of the power of unions, again independent of the human capital of individual union members.

Though widespread discrimination has long characterized the practices of organized labor (Hill 1977, 1982) minorities have also benefited from the equalizing effect that unions have had on the distribution of wealth between capital and labor (Freeman and Medoff 1984). Contrary to the assertion of human-capital theory that discrimination hurts employers, economist Michael Reich found that employer profits were larger, inequality among all workers was more extensive, and racial inequality was more pronounced in those cities where unions were weaker. In other words, workers, particularly black workers, benefit—at the expense of employers—where unions are strongest (Reich 1981). Two key conclusions emerge from this study. Racial inequality and inequality among all workers go hand in hand, and power is critical in determining wage levels generally and racial disparities in particular. These findings are particularly important given the deindustrialization of America that has occurred since the late 1960s.

The role of government at all levels, but particularly the federal government, in determining wage levels is another important factor that the neoclassical paradigm ignores. Relations among capital, labor, and government influence the level and distribution of the costs and benefits of tax expenditures, government contracts and guaranteed loans, tariffs, inheritance laws, minimum wage, labor law and civil rights enforcement, and other factors that dramatically alter the context within which labor markets presumably clear. In efforts to assure private capital accumulation while providing legitimacy for the resulting inequalities—and to preserve their own positions—public officials *do* shape wage levels in ways that are responsive to a range of messages, in addition to the signals of the market (O'Conner 1973; Lindblom 1977; Reed 1988). Recent debates over industrial policy and the competitiveness of the American economy are simply more visible manifestations of what has long been a central role of politics in shaping the U.S. economy, urban redevelopment initiatives and the opportunity structure for various participants (Judd 1984; Reich 1983, 1992).

The political economy perspective offers perhaps the most sweeping critique of the neoclassical paradigm, particularly human-capital theory. There are important commonalities, though, in the various challenges to what still remains the dominant perspective. Where neoclassical economists see individuals competing in an efficiency-maximizing, unitary market on the basis of particular skills developed as a result of voluntary career choices, ultimately for the benefit of society generally, their critics see groups of people and institutions operating in a segmented and often exploitative environment using collective tactics to further what are frequently conflicting interests. The former perspective sees a free market with appropriate education and training as the key to ending racial discrimination; the latter calls for changes in those structural characteristics of the economy and society generally that perpetuate such discrimination.

Employee Ownership, Equality and Equal Opportunity

In light of what has been learned about the structural determinants of racial inequality, the organizational characteristics of many employee-owned firms may suggest approaches that can be taken to better understand the dynamics of racial inequalities and to ameliorate them. The principal characteristic of many employee-owned firms that is conducive to smaller racial inequalities than in conventionally structured firms is the existence of a conscious effort to provide for a more equal distribution of resources, responsibility, and revenues among all employees. This is accomplished through a variety of policies and practices.

Management perquisites, such as executive parking lots and lunchrooms, are frequently eliminated (Rosen, Klein, and Young 1986, 10). Employees often participate in what have traditionally been considered management responsibilities, including sitting on boards of directors. In some cases, employees own and control all phases of the operation. Special training programs are sometimes implemented to prepare workers for tasks they have not previously performed. Job rotation programs may be implemented to give workers experience in various operations. New job ladders may be created to facilitate upward mobility. The responsibilities of individual jobs may be changed so that each position will entail more diverse responsibilities, thus reducing the rigidity of the division of labor and providing for a more egalitarian job structure. In some firms, a cap is set on the maximum allowable difference between the salaries given to the highest and lowest paid employees. Profits are often distributed equally among all employees. When business is slow, employee-owned firms are less likely to lay off workers and are more likely to temporarily reduce wages of all employees or accept lower profits (Russell 1985,

61–64). In the insurance company referred to above, no employee can earn more than five times the salary of the lowest paid worker compared to a seventeen-fold average difference industry-wide, temporary salary reductions among all are accepted as an alternative to layoffs, workers have management responsibilities, training is available to prepare workers for those responsibilities, and several other policies have been implemented to provide for what the company refers to as "its own participatory democracy" (Mariam 1985).

Many of these practices do upgrade the human capital of employees, but it is the structural changes that permit such upgrading and, more importantly, which account for the egalitarian effects. These kinds of policies are not unique to employee-owned businesses, of course, but they are more prevalent in such settings.

Preliminary analysis of one set of companies with employee stock ownership plans further suggests the egalitarian effects of democratically structured work organizations. In examining thirty-seven ESOPs for which data were available, racial income disparities were found to be smaller in those firms that had created formal worker-participation groups (i.e., groups designed to involve nonmanagerial employees in selected management decisionmaking areas pertaining to production) than in those firms which had not created such groups. In addition, where workers had input into pay, hiring and firing decisions, wage disparities between whites and nonwhites were smaller (Squires and Lyson 1991).

To the extent that employee ownership and the associated personnel practices change the structural characteristics that have blocked opportunities for racial minorities (e.g., expand responsibilities and rewards for lower level jobs to increase the number of primary sector jobs and reduce the number of secondary jobs, create job ladders linking lower and higher level positions, or enhance the position of labor relative to management) and alter the power relationships that have denied opportunities to these groups (e.g., provide employee representation—if not control—on boards of directors or redistribute management responsibility among workers), the concept of employee ownership can be a valuable tool for ameliorating racial inequalities in the U.S. labor market. None of this suggests that macroeconomic policy, education, training, and human capital are unimportant, particularly in a global postindustrial society in which knowledge will be a vital avenue of upward mobility for many (Reich 1992; Marshall and Tucker 1992). The opportunity for racial minorities to obtain the necessary human capital, however, will itself depend on structural changes in political and economic institutions. To focus on human capital variables, at the exclusion of the various structural characteristics of the labor market that shape racial inequalities, would ignore much of what is now known theoretically and empirically about the causes of those inequalities, and therefore would lead to ineffective public policy.

Employee ownership and the types of egalitarian personnel policies cited above are not implemented primarily, if at all, for the purpose of ameliorating racial inequality, although many employee-owned firms have implemented affirmative action plans. Given the concentration of racial minorities among the lower rungs of the American occupational structure, though, any efforts to reduce inequality generally will facilitate efforts to alter the relative position of racial minorities.

Civil Rights and Beyond

If an urban policy is to address the issue of racial inequality in the nation's cities effectively, traditional civil rights struggles must be complemented with efforts that will democratize the nation's economic institutions. Enactment of a series of laws prohibiting employment discrimination, an increase in black elected officials and expression of more tolerant racial attitudes by whites do not mean that "the battle for civil rights was fought and won," as some suggest (Sowell 1984, 109). If the federal government has led the way to significant civil rights victories in recent years, it must be recalled that, historically, the federal government, has been a fickle friend of black freedom struggles. The institution of slavery was sanctioned by the federal government with the Supreme Court confirming its constitutionality in the Dred Scott decision. A decade of reconstruction was followed by withdrawal of federal troops (and with them the protections granted by the Civil War amendments) and the onset of the infamous "black codes." Not until Franklin D. Roosevelt issued a series of executive orders banning discrimination in the nation's defense industries did the federal government again act positively on civil rights concerns.

If the 1960s constituted a decade of progressive action by two presidents and their administrations, the retreat of the 1980s showed how fragile that posture can be. The favorable affirmative action decisions by the Supreme Court in 1986 and 1987, followed by the setbacks in 1989, are additional reminders of that fragility. Vital political victories of the civil rights movement over the past three decades do remain intact, but they provide tools to build with, not laurels to rest upon. Proliferation of employee ownership may constitute one direction in which to work.

If the implementation of employee ownership and the egalitarian personnel policies frequently associated with this form of ownership enhance the relative earnings of racial minorities, one obvious conclusion is that the proliferation of such policies will enable more minorities to assume greater responsibilities, earn more money, and contribute more to the development of their families and communities. In turn, these conclusions suggest tactics that would enable organizations to take better advantage of the talents that racial minorities can bring to the workplace. The U.S. economy would gain from the enhanced productivity of these individuals and organizations.

If employee ownership reduces wage disparities associated with race, the particular policies that appear most responsible for that outcome would suggest tactics that employers could use voluntarily, civil rights officials might use in their enforcement efforts, and economic development professionals could incorporate in their work. Redesigning job responsibilities, rotating jobs, creating new jobs ladders, providing additional training, decentralizing authority, sharing burdens of unemployment (thus mitigating the "last hired, first fired" syndrome), capping wage differentials, sharing profits, and flattening employment hierarchies generally are, in fact, already advocated by many equal employment opportunity consultants and utilized in some affirmative action plans (Kanter 1977, 265–303; U.S. Commission on Civil Rights 1981, 43–56; Thomas 1991). One critical advantage of these approaches is that they do not necessarily involve the kinds of numerical goals, timetables, or quotas that have been the subject of such heated controversy for more than twenty years (Glazer 1975; Ryan 1982; Leadership Conference on Civil Rights 1985; Carter 1991; Ezorsky 1991; Urofsky 1991; Taylor 1991; Orlans and O'Neill 1992).

Employee ownership is viewed as an increasingly attractive approach to economic development by a broad spectrum of the U.S. population. Equal opportunity is a firmly established value in American culture, though disputes rage over how to achieve it. Proliferation of employee ownership, at least certain forms, may provide paths for addressing two of the nation's most pressing, divisive, and increasingly interdependent problems—economic stagnation and discrimination—but in a manner that builds on sources of consensus that prevail in American society while minimizing points of contention and conflict.

The form and location of ownership, however, is critical. As indicated above, in the absence of meaningful democratic control, employee ownership can lead to lower wages, more subtle yet more effective manipulation and control of workers and increasing economic risk as all eggs are concentrated in one basket, and a possibly leaking one at that. Employees could be caught up in interfirm competition and lose sight of their common interests as workers and conflicts that remain with management. Therefore, such developments within individual work settings must be complemented with labor law reform that would prohibit permanent replacement of striking workers; provide mandatory bargaining over product quality, marketing, pricing, and other issues traditionally reserved for management; and more efficient and effective National Labor Relations Board procedures to protect the right to organize and prevent unfair labor practices including unequal representation of racial minorities by their unions (Rothstein 1993).

If employee ownership is perceived simply as a temporary bailout for failing businesses, few benefits are likely to be realized. Feasibility studies, market analyses, and sound business planning generally are as essential for these kinds of entrepreneurial ventures as for any other investment. Such technical assistance is increasingly available through organizations like the New York Center for Employee Ownership, the Midwest Center for Labor Research in Chicago, the Employee Ownership Center in Detroit, and the National Center for Employee Ownership in Oakland.

Experiences with more democratic formulations of employee ownership suggest the potential of the establishment of more egalitarian workplace organizations as one tactic for ameliorating racial inequality and enhancing the productivity of the local economy. Commitment to preserving jobs and local communities, characteristics of many employee-owned businesses (and locally owned firms with various types of ownership structures), make such businesses important contributors to local economic development efforts, which should translate into increasing opportunities for the racial minorities concentrated in the nation's major urban communities.

None of this suggests that employee ownership, in and of itself, can resolve the serious economic problems that plague the U.S. economy, its cities, and particularly its minority population. Nor does this suggest any reduction in voluntary affirmative action planning or civil rights enforcement. What this does suggest is that, as part of a much broader effort to confront changing economic realities and develop appropriate democratic responses, there may be some additional tools, or new twists on some old tools, that might be considered in the urban redevelopment and civil rights arenas. As Barry Bluestone and Irving Bluestone argue:

> [T]he cornerstone in the rebuilding of America lies in reshaping the fundamental relationship between employees and management and creating a new work culture. Appropriate fiscal and monetary policies and adequate investment in advanced technology are necessary preconditions for an American economic renaissance, along with investments in public infrastructure, education, and training.
>
> We contend that no matter how fine-tuned these macro policies, the nation's economic engine will not run smoothly until relations in

the workplace are radically and democratically reorganized. (Bluestone and Bluestone 1992, xiii)

The racial disparities found by the Kerner Commission in 1968 in such critical economic areas as income, unemployment and labor-force participation persist today. This hardly suggests, however, that the U.S. labor market has remained unaltered. The American economy, its cities and the structure of opportunity confronting blacks have changed dramatically since 1968. It is no longer sufficient, if it ever was, to simply address the allocation of various groups across the occupational distributions of American employers or the human capital accumulated by the U.S. work force. Macro level economic policy decisions and the internal structural characteristics of individual economic organizations must become the focus of public policy in civil rights as well as economic development arenas. The public costs of private enterprise for far too many American families and communities have become too great to abdicate fundamental investment and economic structural decisionmaking to private authorities alone.

Injecting a strong dose of democracy into the nation's economic institutions is essential to remedying the diverse problems confronting those most vulnerable to the vagaries of uneven development. Just more of what was demanded in the 1960s will not be adequate for the nation's cities and their minority populations during the remainder of this century and beyond.

If the individualistic assumptions of human-capital theory and traditional explanations for racial inequalities in the labor market fail to explain those inequalities or provide a sound base for policy, similar blinders shape housing policy. Housing and employment, of course, are highly intertwined. Many of the structural changes that have altered the nature of work have also dramatically influenced housing policy and practice. One consequence is the perpetuation, and in some cases exacerbation, of racial inequalities in the nation's housing market, the subject of the next chapter.

3

All the Discomforts of Home: The Politics and Economics of Housing

No man who owns his own house and lot can be a Communist. He has too much to do.

William Levitt, 1948 (Jackson 1985:231)

The poet Robert Frost once observed that "Home is the place where, when you have to go there, they have to let you in" (Jackson 1985, 73). As Frost clearly understood, housing is far more than brick and mortar. While housing provides protection from the elements, when people rent or purchase housing they are obtaining far more than physical shelter. At home, one can usually get away from the pressures of work, intrusive neighbors (even in-laws on occasion), and many of the tensions of daily life. The selection of a particular home also requires the selection of a neighborhood and all the amenities it does or does not have. Housing determines the quality of schools children will attend. The quality of other public services including police and fire protection, recreation, and transportation is shaped by housing choices. The nature of one's friends and degree of interaction with them can be determined by housing. Access to jobs is often heavily influenced by access to housing. In addition to these concrete lifestyle considerations, more abstract but equally important determinants of the quality of life including social status and personal identity are shaped by and intersect with housing.

Along with the consumption of housing, the production and distribution of housing are preeminently social phenomena. But housing has rarely been subject to sociological research. The analysis of housing has generally been treated as an economic matter viewed through the prism of self-regulating free market neoclassical economic theory. Individual producers and consumers meet in the marketplace where voluntary transactions are carried out constrained only by the tastes and financial limitations of the buyers. Even when sociology has turned its attention to housing, it has generally been with the same individualistic, voluntaristic tools. As Nathan Glazer wrote, "We deal with a market of millions of individual purchasers and hundreds of thousands of individual suppliers. . . . The purchase or rental of housing involves an individual choice limited by an economic capacity" (Glazer 1975, 134–35). But the emphasis has been on individual choice rather than factors affecting economic capacity. Indeed, it is largely because of the widespread acceptance of the individualistic assumptions surrounding housing that severe housing problems persist and policymakers are so often frustrated in their efforts to find solutions (Gilderbloom and Applebaum 1988).

A divergent perspective has emerged in recent years which focuses more on the institutional framework in which housing choices are made and less on the exchanges between individual housing consumers and providers. This chapter examines the nature and role of housing in urban America, focusing on the mutually reinforcing dynamics of housing and uneven development. By examining the institutional structure of housing, the broader economic and political forces in which it is embedded, and, therefore, the context framing individual housing consumption choices, a more comprehensive understanding of housing and an array of social problems associated with housing can be developed. Hopefully, such an understanding can lead to the resolution of what often appear to be unresolvable problems of housing and inequality in many of the nation's urban communities.

The following pages describe key facets of the housing industry and many of the housing problems currently facing growing numbers of families in the United States. The unequal impact of housing policy and practice particularly in terms of the uneven spatial development of cities and the exacerbation of racial inequalities, are examined. Foreseeable problems are identified, specific research proposals are suggested to develop further an understanding of emerging housing related problems, and directions are proposed for policies that can ameliorate what has already become one of the most difficult challenges confronting urban America, simply housing the citizenry.

Housing: A Matter of Consumption, Production, and Distribution

Housing does provide protection from the elements, but it does so unevenly, and not simply in response to the vagaries of a free market. Class, race, gender, and several related political factors shape the quality of that shelter and, as the growing homeless population demonstrates, whether or not any shelter at all is available. Even more evident is the unequal consumption of the amenities associated with the acquisition of a home. But the limitations of the individualistic/voluntaristic approach are particularly evident in examining the production and distribution of housing.

The housing industry, or more specifically the particular industries that are involved in the production and distribution of housing, are significant economic actors. Contractors, homebuilders, lenders, insurers, appraisers, real estate agents, and others represent a variety of wealthy and powerful economic organizations that employ millions of people and control trillions of dollars. For example, in 1989 the insurance industry employed over two million people and controlled assets totaling more than $1.8 trillion (*Insurance Information Institute* 1991). Thrift institutions (primarily those lenders previously known as savings and loans) employed more than 400,000 people and controlled $1.5 trillion. The industry with the largest concentration of wealth, commercial banks, controlled $3.3 trillion (*Savings Institutions Sourcebook* 1990). The structure, and current restructuring, of housing related industries dramatically affects the availability and cost of housing. To acknowledge that significant economic institutions shape the distribution of housing, however, is not to suggest that they do so principally through the free-market vision of neoclassical economics.

In part because of their economic size, these industries are also key political actors who use their clout to influence the production, distribution, and consumption of housing. The large presence of housing-related lobbyists in Washington, D.C. symbolizes how politics affects the economics of housing. Over 600 firms and trade associations, representing lenders, builders, contractors, and insurers, have offices in the nation's capital (Close et al. 1991). Some of these are major employers in their own right. The American Bankers Association (ABA), for example, has a staff of 400 and a budget of $62 million. Responsibilities of the ABA include "liaison with federal bank regulators . . . submits draft legislation and lobbies Congress on issues affecting commercial banks . . . files briefs and lawsuits in major court cases affecting the industry" (Burek 1991, 54). The U.S. League of Savings Institutions, with a staff of 441, "promotes the improvement of statutes and regulations affecting the savings institution business and the public interest" (Burek 1991, 60). The American Insurance Association (AIA) employs a staff of 150 people on a budget of $20 million in its Washington office, and the insurance industry is regulated primarily by state governments. The AIA "represents members' interests before state and federal legislative and regulatory bodies" (Burek 1991, 214). Such political representation is one reason why housing-related industries have secured special privileges (e.g., government insurance of deposits and loan products, deduction of property taxes and mortgage loan interest payments from federal income taxes, exemption of the insurance industry from federal regulation), and why the free market model is simply inappropriate for understanding housing.

The various economic and political dimensions of housing-related activities have been conducted in accordance with a reasonably coherent ideological framework rooted in the ideology of privatism. It is a framework which, at one level, extols the virtues of individualism and entrepreneurship but, in effect, nurtures and reinforces collective (particularly corporate) interests and structural inequalities. As with development activity generally, (discussed in chapter 5) housing policy has been predicated on the assumptions that productivity is generated primarily by the individual pursuit of material well-being, that free markets provide the most efficient mechanism for pursuing production and development, and if government has a role it is to supplement and enhance the process and outcome of the private market (Hays 1985). Consequently, housing policy and practice both reflect and reinforce key trajectories of social inequality. Specifically, the production, distribution, and consumption of housing are shaped by uneven spatial development of metropolitan areas and the dynamics of race relations. In turn, housing policy and practice foster uneven development and racial stratification.

The emerging institutional (political economy) perspective on housing provides a more coherent theoretical framework for understanding the history, contemporary role and problems, and options for future policy in housing than had previously evolved from the ecological perspective in urban research and mainstream neoclassical theory in general. If no single source or statement serves as the ultimate authority for this theoretical perspective, a rough consensus has emerged from many directions on central tenets that has advanced contemporary understanding of housing and urban development (examples include Lefebvre 1992; Harvey 1985; Gottdiener 1985; Castells 1983; Gottdiener and Feagin 1988; Feagin and Smith 1987; Fainstein et al. 1986).

Perhaps the most critical distinction between these two paradigms is that the institutional approach views as problematic vital social processes and relationships that the mainstream perspective long ignored or accepted as a given or inevitable, if not benevolent, feature of American society. One vivid example is the process of private capital accumulation and the unequal, often exploitative, social relations embedded in that process. Instead of assuming the benevolence of the "creative destruction" of capitalism, the emerging institutional approach has demonstrated the destabilizing and, for many people, the permanent debilitating effects of market-based investment practices. Housing, as a central part of the economy and consumer culture, is hardly immune to these developments.

A second related dynamic is the process of urban restructuring and, most significantly, the local effects of national and international economic as well as political development. If concentric circles still ring Chicago, they reflect that city's role in a global system of cities as much as the decisions of boss Daley's son, the Chicago Association of Commerce and Industry, and the hundreds of community organizations in that city of neighborhoods.

Third is the key role of government and politics generally in shaping the life of the city including the nature of housing and housing problems. At all levels of government, political decisions affect the quality and quantity of the production and distribution of housing. It is precisely for this reason that major actors in the private housing industry devote so much attention to government activity.

Given the central role of housing in the political economy of urban America, it is inevitable that housing has become intertwined with broader efforts to facilitate capital accumulation while, at the same time, providing legitimization for the unequal and inequitable outcomes of that process. Housing, related real estate development, and those activities Harvey (1985) describes as forming the secondary circuit of capital, have become major pieces of local and regional economies, thus bringing major private housing industry actors into the political arena at all levels. As indicated above, public subsidies for housing have enriched producers within that industry and they have favored wealthy consumers over low- or middle-income families. But subsidies for home ownership have also been offered in an effort to ameliorate the contradiction noted by Stone (1986) between the rising costs of housing necessary to support that market with the depressed level of wages required to maintain the labor market. If a degree of legitimization has been achieved through the expansion of home ownership—if in fact a homeowner has no time for Communism—fundamental conflicts remain and, as discussed below, the prevalence of home ownership itself is now threatened.

One outcome of these developments is the increasing commodification of urban space itself (Gottdiener 1985) and emerging conflicts between those who view the city and their neighborhood for its use value (as a place to live, work, and play) versus those who are primarily concerned with the exchange value of property (as opportunity for investment and profitmaking) (Logan and Molotch 1987). How this conflict is being played out reflects important structural features—including the ecology—of local communities, but also the conscious political acts of the people who are affected.

The production, distribution, and consumption of housing cannot be understood simply or primarily as the outcome of the voluntary choices of random individuals in a free market. In fact housing represents the interplay of powerful institutions which do interact with millions of individuals, but in a manner that reflects and reinforces various trajectories of inequality, most notably those associated with class, space, and race. The built environment constitutes an integral part of the process of capital accumulation, not just the physical surroundings in which, through the production and distribution of goods and services, that process is played out (Lamarche 1976).

The sociologist Louis Wirth wrote over forty-five years ago that "civilization can be judged, at least to some extent, by the minimum housing conditions which a society will tolerate for its members" (Wirth 1947, 139). In light of the highly unequal distribution of housing and the amenities associated with housing, a perspective that reflects the central structural underpinnings of housing (e.g., the process of private capital accumulation, urban restructuring, and the political response) is vital if that judgment is to be knowledgeably made, and even more important if policies are to be found to elevate that civilization.

Ideology, Policy, and Housing

Housing has long been a subject of prominent domestic policy debate. Throughout this century several major pieces of housing legislation have been enacted with several noble stated objectives. For example, the U.S. Housing Act of 1937 was enacted in part "to remedy the unsafe and insanitary housing conditions and the acute shortage of decent, safe, and sanitary dwellings for families of low income in rural or urban communities that are injurious to the health, safety, and morals of the nation." The 1949 Housing Act called for "the realization as soon as feasible of the goal of a decent home and a suitable living environment for every American family." The Federal Fair Housing Act of 1968 was motivated by a desire to "replace the nation's ghettos with truly balanced and integrated living patterns." And the 1974 Housing and Community Development Act called for "the development of viable urban communities by providing decent housing and a suitable living environment and expanding economic opportunities principally for persons of low and moderate income." While there have been improvements in the physical quality of the nation's housing stock during these years, in the 1980s many housing related problems became more severe.

The proportion of housing units defined as substandard or overcrowded has declined dramatically over the past fifty years. However, a significant number of families, over 5 percent (in a total of 7.4 million occupied housing units) according to the U.S. Census Bureau's 1985 Annual Housing Survey, contained "moderate or severe physical problems." More significantly, these problems were very unevenly distributed. For example, 20 percent of black homeowners and 30 percent of black households below the poverty level lived in housing units with such problems. The number of families living in overcrowded units (more than one person per room) has increased in recent years, from 1.2 million in 1975 to 1.5 million in 1985. In 1980 less than 5 percent of white households compared to 15 percent of black households and 30 percent of Korean households resided in overcrowded housing units (Zarembka 1990).

Affordability problems have increased dramatically in recent years. For renters housing costs increased twice as fast as incomes between 1970 and 1983 with the proportion spending at least 25 percent of their income on rent increasing from 40 to 59 percent of all renters. Again, this burden did not fall equally on all groups. Over 80 percent of households with incomes under $10,000 paid more than one-quarter of their income for housing compared to just two percent of those earning $50,000 or more. Homeowners were not spared from affordability problems. During these years the cost of housing (sale price and mortgage payments) increased four and one-half times (Applebaum 1989, 316–17). Consequently, the rate of homeownership declined during the 1980s for the first time since 1940. In 1980 65.6 percent of families owned the home in which they lived, but in 1986 this figure dropped to 63.8 percent (Zarembka 1990, 8).

One consequence of the growing affordability problems is the dramatic increase in displacement and homelessness. Estimates of homelessness range from several hundred thousand to three million. In any case, the number is much higher today than a decade earlier and an increasing proportion of the homeless consists of families, working poor people who cannot afford housing, and victims of gentrification and other forms of displacement. Homelessness, in other words, is not just a problem for drug addicts, the mentally ill, and others with physical or mental impairments (Zarembka 1990, 7, 12).

A continuing feature of the nation's housing markets is racial segregation. Despite passage of the Federal Fair Housing Act in 1968, between 1970 and 1990 the extent of segregation between blacks and whites in major metropolitan areas declined only slightly, particularly in the north, with indexes of dissimilarity in the larger cities exceeding .7 in most cases and northern cities still averaging closer to .8. This means that 70 percent or 80 percent of all blacks or whites in most U.S. cities would have to move in order to achieve a totally integrated pattern where the percentage of both groups in each census tract would reflect their representation in the metropolitan area as a whole. For blacks these patterns hold for high income as well as low income families. In fact, no matter how socioeconomic status is measured (e.g., education, occupation) segregation indices for blacks remain high while those for Hispanics and Asians fall as status rises (Massey and Denton 1987; 1993, 61–67, 83–88, 221–23). The U.S. Department of Housing and Urban Development (HUD) estimates there are two million instances of housing discrimination occurring every year (Schwemm 1989, 272). A national audit of housing practices by the Urban Institute found that black and Hispanic homeseekers experience discrimination in over half their encounters with real estate agents (Turner et al. 1991, vi, 37).

Public response to these problems suggests at least part of the causes. Over two-thirds of the more than 7.5 million tenant households with incomes below the poverty line in 1985 neither lived in public housing nor received any housing aid. Budget authority for non-Indian conventional public housing decreased from $4.2 billion in 1981 to $573 million in 1988 and the number of new additional public housing units decreased from 18,003 in 1981 to 3,109 in 1988. During these years the federal tax revenues lost due to deductions for mortgage interest and property taxes grew from $25 billion to $50 billion, a benefit that goes primarily to upper income families (Zarembka 1990, 1, 18). In 1984, for example, these two subsidies cost the Treasury $49.4 billion, more than HUD has spent on all of its housing assistance programs since the beginning of public housing in 1937 (Applebaum 1989, 319).

The uneven nature of the nation's housing problems flows logically from the privatistic ideology that has dominated housing policy. As indicated above, there are three central contentions of that dominant ideology: (1) the basic force that drives human productivity is the desire of individuals to enhance their material well-being and to be recognized for their success through the competitive process, therefore society must reward acquisitiveness and competitiveness in order to maximize overall material well being; (2) the free market is the most effective and least coercive mechanism for allocating goods and services since it harmonizes individual self-interest with society's collective development; and (3) government's role is to reinforce and supplement the market in regulating exchange in a manner that maximizes individual freedom and choice (Hays 1985, 17, 18). In essence, given their "proven" abilities, it is in the interest of society generally for housing policy to assist the winners in the marketplace.

While housing industry leaders and their partners in government have persistently celebrated the glories of the free market, the public sector has long had a central role. Tax deductions for mortgage interest and property taxes enable homeowners to purchase more expensive housing than they could otherwise afford, thus subsidizing contractors, lenders, insurers, and everyone else involved in housing. Highway construction paid for by federal tax dollars opened up the suburbs and created space for more housing development than would have otherwise taken place. Subsidies for mass transit have had similar effects. Federal insurance of many mortgage loan products provide additional public support. Even public housing and other programs to support low-income families provide governmental aid for many in the housing industry. In most low-income programs providers charge what they determine to be a fair market price, the consumers pay what the government determines to be an affordable share of their incomes, and the government pays the difference. Subsidies to the poor become, in effect, subsidies to the winners in the marketplace (Hays 1985, 28).

This ideological approach to housing is vividly portrayed in *The Report of The President's Commission on Housing* which was released in 1982. President Reagan created this commission to develop strategies for addressing many of the nation's housing and related community development needs. Among the charges given to the commission was the following, "seek to develop housing and mortgage finance options which strengthen the ability of the private sector to maximize opportunities for homeownership and provide adequate shelter for all Americans" (President's Commission on Housing 1982, xv). It is interesting to note that the charge was *not* to maximize opportunities for homeownership and adequate shelter, but rather to "strengthen the ability of the private sector" to attempt to achieve these objective. The report goes on to ask "How can the private market expand housing opportunities?" (xv) and to argue "Government's role should emphasize individual freedom of choice" (xvi). The commission states that it "approached its task with optimism based on . . . the genius of the market economy" (xvii) and concluded the "goals are most likely to be achieved if government shrewdly encourages rather than suspiciously controls the exercise of private initiative through the spectrum of activities that produce the homes in which we live" (xviii).

Given that the ideological perspective shaping housing policy advocates enhancing the opportunities of those who succeed in the marketplace, it is not surprising that the outcome has been a series of housing-related policies that reflect and reinforce various dimensions of social inequality. In light of the close connection between housing and community development policy, it is also unsurprising that unequal access to housing is intricately linked with the uneven spatial development of cities.

Housing and the Uneven Development of Urban America

Uneven development, in terms of the industrial and spatial configuration of cities and the outcomes of this process as it effects class, race, and gender groups within cities, has been the predominant feature of the evolution of metropolitan areas in the United States in recent decades, if not throughout the nation's history. Perhaps the most significant prophecy of recent times was the warning of the Kerner Commission report noted earlier that continuation of present policies would permanently divide the nation into two societies polarized along class, spatial, and racial lines (*Report of the National Advisory Commission on Civil Disorders* 1968, 22). In the years following this report, little has happened to challenge this pessimistic prediction. Between 1970 and 1990 suburban communities have been growing much faster than central cities, increasing their proportion of the total metropolitan population from under 55 percent to over 60 percent. The black portion of the central city population increased from 21 percent to 23 percent compared to an increase from 5 percent to 7 percent in the suburban ring (O'Hare et al. 1991, 9). During these years the majority of the population in several of the nation's largest cities became nonwhite (e.g., Detroit, Washington, D.C., Atlanta, St. Louis), while a significant portion of the growing black suburban population reflected the expansion of segregated nonwhite communities across city lines, the impoverishment of small and predominantly black cities near big cities like Camden and East St. Louis, and the expansion of suburban boundaries to include poor formerly rural black families, rather than desegregation (Massey and Denton 1993, 67–74). And median family income in the nation's cities fell from over 78 percent of the suburban median to under 69 percent (U.S. Bureau of the Census 1970, 1992).

In many critical respects, divisions between cities and suburbs are far greater than these numbers suggest. For example, in 1988–89 per student spending in public schools varied from just $5,265 in Chicago to $9,371 in suburban Niles Township. In New Jersey the gap was even greater between Camden where the per pupil expenditure was $3,538 compared to $7,725 in Princeton. This pattern is replicated in cities throughout the country (Kozol 1991). Many of the wealthiest families in urban areas, of course, have opted out of the public schools entirely. And as Robert Reich (1991) suggests, families in the top 20% of the income distribution (who make more than the remaining four-fifths put together) are seceding from the rest of the nation in more ways than the schools to which they send their children. Public parks deteriorate as the wealthy join private health, tennis, skating, country, and other clubs of all sorts. Many suburban developments and even individual homeowners purchase their own police protection as the number of private security guards in the United States now exceeds the number of public police officers. The spatial patterns of cities clearly reflect the emerging socioeconomic disparities.

Economic restructuring, nurtured by government policy, reinforced this basic pattern of urban development. While downtown central business districts and some residential areas have experienced a renaissance in many metropolitan areas and suburban communities have flourished, this development has often come at the expense of inner ring blue-collar industrial and residential communities, resulting in what *Chicago Tribune* columnist Clarence Page labeled a "dumbbell economy" (Page 1987). The decline of manufacturing plants and jobs coupled with the rise in both high-skilled, high-wage professional service positions and low- skilled, low-paid service jobs have been major contributors to the uneven spatial development of cities. Downtown office and entertainment centers serve the growing service industries and the surrounding suburbs house the higher paid employees and their families (Kasarda 1988; Bluestone and Harrison 1988; Wilson 1987). The lower paid and unemployed are trapped in between spatially, while they are pushed further down socially and economically. The growth in both high-wage and low-wage jobs are not separate processes but rather parts of the same dynamic. Industries employing large numbers of highly paid professional workers also employ many low-paid clerical and unskilled service workers. The increasing number of highly paid professionals in major metropolitan areas also creates demands for low-wage unskilled workers to provide personal services (as waiters in restaurants, sales clerks in boutiques, and security guards in fortress-style housing developments) demanded by the new urban gentry (Sassen 1991). The cultural capital created as part of the gentrification process generally, therefore, both reflects and reinforces this duality (Zukin 1991).

Given the individualistic assumptions of neoclassical economics and the dominant privatistic ideology in which that perspective is grounded, it is not surprising that public policy has responded to prevailing economic problems by offering a variety of incentives to private enterprises (e.g., tax reductions and abatements, low-interest loans, relief from government regulations) in efforts to create a more attractive "business climate" in hopes that communities could attract mobile capital and grow out of their economic doldrums. Such supply side approaches generated little economic growth and exacerbated prevailing inequalities (Mishel and Frankel 1991). Urban policy, which has flown under several banners (e.g., urban renewal, model cities, public-private partnership—see chapter 5 for a more detailed discussion) has reinforced in spatial terms the economic and social inequalities rooted in private investment practices. The concentration of poverty and various dimensions of social pathology that have emerged in recent years, particularly in central city neighborhoods, reflect these private sector investment practices and public policy initiatives (Fainstein et al. 1986).

Housing policy during these years reflected and reinforced these patterns. The flight from central cities to the suburbs is conventionally explained as an outcome of consumer sovereignty in the housing market. Seeking an escape from the ills of urban life and preferring a more wholesome environment in which to raise their children, increasingly affluent families sought out larger, more private, and more comfortable homes in the suburbs. Not only are such homes perceived as providing a better quality of life, but they also constitute a better investment. While these consumer preferences played a significant role in the growth of the suburbs and decline of central cities, this general characterization is, at best, one-sided and fails to take into consideration the role of structural forces, emergent cultural values, and major institutional actors, particularly real estate developers and related housing industries, with substantial assistance from the federal government (Checkoway 1986; Judd 1984; Feagin and Parker 1989). As Checkoway concluded, "Suburbanization prevailed because of the decisions of large operators and powerful economic institutions supported by federal government programs, ordinary consumers had little real choice in the basic pattern that resulted" (Checkoway 1986, 134).

The availability of cheap land, support from the federal government, and growing demand for housing following World War II, presented opportunities for real estate developers and, through the construction and sale of single family homes, huge economic opportunities for homebuilders, lenders, property insurers, and other housing-related industries. Larger developers, like Levitt and Sons who built more than 17,000 identical homes in one Long Island development subsequently known as "Levittown," typified the forces primarily responsible for the emerging spatial development of metropolitan areas. While many consumers, no doubt, wanted such housing, it is also evident that those preferences were shaped by the marketing practices of the housing industry. The American dream was sold as much as it was bought. And it was not just the amenities of suburban living that were sold. Suburban living was sold as a reward that "successful" people and their family deserved and that living in suburban neighborhoods reflected a higher morality on the part of the homeowner as well as his neighbors. The following advertisements for suburban housing developments built in the 1950s illustrate the selling of the American dream:

> When you settle at East Hempstead you are "on the right side of the tracks" in more ways than one. It's the hub of Long Island's most desirable residential section. . . .
> The Cedar Hill Ranch Home, frankly, wasn't designed for the man in the street. There are many homes costing less that ably satisfy his needs. The size and appointments of Cedar Hill were fashioned for the family who considers anything less than the best inadequate. . . .
> Yes, Cedar Hill was definitely designed for the family accustomed to finer things. (Judd 1984, 169)

Federal housing policy has reinforced the patterns and practices of private housing industries. Working through their trade associations like the National Association of Homebuilders, the National Association of Realtors, the Associated General Contractors, the American Bankers Association, the U.S. League of Savings Institutions, and many others, housing-related industries have for over fifty years secured federal housing policies that focus on the provision of low-interest loans, mortgage interest subsidies, rent supplements, and other market-based inducements. Lobbyists have successfully kept public housing to a minimum in the United States (approximately 3% of all housing), labeling it as "socialistic" and, therefore, un-American. Again, it is the winners in the competitive market that have been the primary beneficiaries of housing policy.

The role of the Federal Housing Administration (FHA) is most illustrative. From the inception of the agency in the 1930s through the 1950s it financed 60% of home purchases, virtually all of which were in suburban communities (Lief and Goering 1987, 229). In a dramatic turn, during the 1960s lenders flooded central city neighborhoods with FHA loans. Given the liberal terms, FHA loans were attractive to lower income families and since all service costs were paid up front and the loans were insured by the federal government, they were attractive to many lenders. Local realtors, who also stood to profit from sales financed with federally insured loans, also took advantage. Consequently, many families purchased homes who were not able to maintain them when repairs became necessary. Massive foreclosures resulted, causing many people to lose their homes and leading directly to the deterioration of many central city neighborhoods. The federal guarantees encouraged many lenders to underwrite their loans less cautiously, discouraged them from providing proper counseling to first-time buyers, and contributed to the destabilization of central city neighborhoods throughout the United States, but at great profit to the housing industry (Bradford 1979).

Other federal policies were also instrumental in encouraging the expansion of suburban housing and discouraging housing in central cities. The massive federally subsidized construction of highways during the postwar years linking downtown central business districts with bedroom suburban communities, often at the expense of central city homes that were razed and families who were displaced, expedited a process that had begun years earlier. Deduction of property taxes and mortgage interest payments subsidized home buyers and housing-related industries. The more expensive the housing, the larger the subsidy. Consequently, suburban communities have benefited most from these public subsidies. The continued development of housing assistance and related housing policy tied to market forces has exacerbated these dimensions of uneven development.

The pro-suburban bias built into these industries has been well documented: appraisers often undervalue central city property; mortgage lenders and insurers redline older urban communities in favor of suburban areas in their underwriting and investment practices (discussed in the following chapter); and real estate agents frequently steer customers (particularly white ones) from urban to suburban housing. If consumer preferences drive some of these decisions, they are preferences that reflect the limited range of choices available in part because of the policies and practices of the housing industry and its policymaking partners in government, and because of the biases of the institutional actors themselves (Tobin 1987; Feldman and Florida 1990; National Commission on Neighborhoods 1979).

Housing policy and practice, in conjunction with economic development policy in general, have fueled the uneven development of metropolitan areas. Housing initiatives stimulated the pro-suburban and anti-urban biases, and once those processes were set in motion public and private sector housing activity has reinforced them. If housing is more attractive in the suburbs, if suburban living is preferred by many because of the schools, job opportunities, and other amenities associated with the suburbs, it is equally clear that consumer preferences alone cannot account for these developments. Structural forces, powerful institutional actors, and the cultural values they propagate have shaped these developments in the past, and they continue to do so today. Nowhere is the mutually reinforcing system of inequality more evident than in the case of race and housing.

Housing and Racial Inequality

When the Kerner Commission warned of the development of two societies, the division it feared would be most problematic was that of race. In the area of housing, no dimension of inequality has been more explicitly or extensively endorsed by private industry and public policymakers than racial inequality. The continuing extensive nature of housing segregation and the widespread practice of racial discrimination in housing noted earlier are grounded in both historical and contemporary utilization of race, and the racial effects of apparently neutral practices by powerful institutional actors in the private housing industry and government.

Housing is one public policy arena where sociology has had an influential, but unfortunate impact. University of Chicago sociologist Homer Hoyt, who advised federal housing officials and private real estate groups, ranked fifteen racial and ethnic groups in terms of their impact on property values in a report he prepared for the Federal Housing Administration in 1933. Those he identified as having the most detrimental effect were Negroes and Mexicans (Hoyt 1933, 315–16). When Hoyt spoke, the FHA listened. In its 1938 *Underwriting Manual* the FHA observed, "If a neighborhood is to retain stability, it is necessary that properties shall continue to be occupied by the same social and racial classes. A change in social or racial occupancy generally contributes to instability and a decline in values" (U.S. Federal Housing Administration 1938, par. 937). The FHA was a leading advocate of racially restrictive covenants which assured that properties would indeed continue to be occupied by members of the same classes. In 1948 the U.S. Supreme Court ruled in the case of *Shelley v. Kramer*, 334 U.S. 1 (1948) that these provisions were unenforceable by the courts, but their effects have lingered.

Appraisers, on whom lenders directly rely and others including insurers and realtors indirectly rely, long held the same world view. Frederick Babcock, a leading theoretician of real estate principles, wrote over fifty years ago: "there is one difference in people, namely race, which can result in very rapid decline. Usually such declines can be partially avoided by segregation and this device has always been in common usage in the South where white and negro populations have been separated" (Babcock 1932, 91). Training materials used by the American Institute of Real Estate Appraisers in the 1970s used the following example to illustrate neighborhood analysis: "The neighborhood is entirely Caucasian. It appears that there is no adverse effect by minority groups" (Greene 1980, 9).

Similarly, the National Association of Realtors included the following advice in its code of ethics until 1950: "A realtor should never be instrumental in introducing into a neighborhood a character of property or occupancy, members of any race or nationality, or any individual whose presence will clearly be detrimental to property values in the neighborhood" (Judd 1984, 284). Racial steering by real estate agents whereby white homeseekers are directed to predominantly white neighborhoods while blacks and other racial minorities are shown homes primarily in integrated or nonwhite areas has proven to be a key institutional force in the perpetuation of the dual housing market (Pearce 1979; Turner et al. 1991).

Lenders, insurers, and other housing finance industries that depend on assessments of appraisers and realtors have shared similar biases. If the explicit utilization of race has declined in recent years (though as the next chapter will show, has not disappeared), the racial effects of historical discrimination and of prevailing apparently neutral policies remain. In the area of mortgage lending, black applicants are rejected twice as often as whites (Canner and Smith 1991, 1992). Studies of the distribution of mortgage loans reveal significant racial disparities that do not disappear even after taking into consideration the effects of income, wealth, property value and condition, neighborhood characteristics, and other socioeconomic factors (Bradbury et al. 1989; Shlay 1989). Even when blacks and whites with identical risk related economic characteristics apply for loans, blacks are 60 percent more likely to be rejected (Munnell et al. 1992). These disparities can be explained, in part, by stereotypical assumptions of many lenders that whites have a greater "pride of ownership" and "homeowners mentality" than blacks (ICF Incorporated 1991). Similar patterns have been found in the distribution of homeowners insurance (Squires and Velez 1987).

Race alone, of course, is not the sole or even the predominant factor driving lending behavior. Indeed given the conditions in some neighborhoods, as David Harvey argued, "banks naturally have good, rational business reasons for not financing mortgages. . . . Given the drive to maximize profits, this decision cannot be regarded as unethical. . . . Consequently it seems impossible to find a policy within the existing economic and institutional framework which is capable of rectifying these conditions" (Harvey 1973, 140). But economic considerations alone clearly do not account entirely for these racial disparities.

Virtually all forms of racial discrimination in housing are illegal today. Yet lax enforcement by regulatory agencies still contributes to these racial patterns. One key limitation is the Federal Fair Housing Law itself as it was enacted in 1968. During the first twenty years under the law HUD was provided only with the authority to seek voluntary settlements of alleged violations. Victims were generally dependent on their own resources or those of sympathetic fair housing organizations to take their cases to court for them. With the Fair Housing Amendments Act of 1988 HUD can now take a case before an administrative law judge who can issue penalties up to $10,000 for the first violation, $25,000 for a second within five years, and $50,000 for subsequent offenses within seven years.

But there are other limitations in law enforcement efforts. Resources allocated to HUD and other regulatory agencies have been limited. Federal agencies have been hesitant to do their own statistical analyses of systemic patterns or to use testing techniques in enforcement. And during the 1980s scarce law enforcement resources were utilized to combat efforts to maintain integrated communities, like Starrett City in New York, rather than to encourage these and related efforts to dismantle the dual housing market (Dane 1989; Schwemm 1989).

Clearly, private housing practice and public housing policy have been predicated, at least in part, on racial inequality. Existing patterns of racial inequality and socially accepted stereotypes associated with race have led to racial inequality in the nation's housing markets. In turn, housing policy and practice have fed back and reinforced broader patterns of racial inequality in American society.

Unequal access to housing leads directly to unequal access to other social and economic necessities and amenities. For most families, the home is their largest investment. If the value of the home is depressed it restricts the accumulation of wealth and the advantages wealth confers. The typical white family controls approximately twelve times the wealth of the typical black family with the home being the major asset held by most. Consequently the economic status of individual minority families and predominantly minority communities is depressed. Such disparities adversely affect the ability of racial minorities to purchase homes in the first place, to benefit from the appreciation of real estate when they are able to buy a home (by, among other things, moving to better and more expensive housing in the future), to secure home improvement loans to enhance the quality and value of their homes, or to utilize their residence as collateral for obtaining home equity loans or loans for any other purpose (e.g., education for children, automobiles, business start-ups).

Housing discrimination also limits access to the many amenities discussed earlier that are associated with one's home. Access to jobs is restricted as the areas of the greatest job growth are generally those where housing for racial minorities is most restricted. Minorities are often denied access to the better schools, which hinders their childrens' future economic opportunities. Racial isolation often limits interaction with, and the development of contacts among, middle-class families, which also reduces future educational and economic opportunities. Segregation is a primary cause of the increasing concentration of black poverty, the deterioration of many inner city neighborhoods, and the so-called underclass behavior that ensues. It has been estimated that a 25% reduction in residential segregation would result in a 12% increase in the median black family income and a reduction of 8% in the poverty rate among black families (DeMarco and Galster 1993, 144). In many ways, unequal housing opportunities reduces opportunities to enjoy the full social, economic, and political rights and benefits of citizenry ("Epilogue" 1987; Massey and Eggers 1990; Massey and Denton 1993).

Ironically, the primary benefit that racial minorities may secure from their home is a temporary sanctuary from the ongoing realities of racial discrimination. As one black corporate executive stated, "The only place it probably does not affect me, I guess, is in my home; specifically, actually, in the interior portions of my home. But outside one's home, it always affects me" (Feagin 1991).

Economic Restructuring, Political Response, and the Social Context of Housing Choice

Concentration, globalization, and stagnation in the productivity growth of key sectors of the U.S. economy in the 1980s and 1990s, along with the political response to such restructuring, have significantly shaped the spatial development of metropolitan areas and the social problems smoldering within them. The housing industry has clearly not been immune to these trends.

Since at least the mid 1970s productivity growth in the United States has stagnated, foreign countries have successfully entered markets previously dominated by U.S. industries particularly in manufacturing, domestic industries have become more highly concentrated and they are increasingly integrated into an international economy (Reich 1983, 1991). The basic response of policymakers to ensuing productivity and profitability problems, at the urging of their partners in private business, has been to deregulate industry, lower business taxes, and assist capital in reducing the social wage. Attacks on labor unions, demands for concessions, and reductions in the welfare state have been part of a broader package justified in the name of creating a better business environment, providing entrepreneurs greater flexibility so they can compete in the emerging international economy, and nurturing productivity growth in general (Bluestone and Harrison 1988).

While failing to stimulate the desired economic growth, this political response to private industry ills has exacerbated the uneven spatial development of metropolitan areas and the associated inequalities of class and race (Mishel and Frankel 1991; Levy 1987; Wilson 1987). Even Republican Party strategist Kevin Phillips warned of looming dangers resulting from the massive concentrations of wealth during the 1980s, which he attributes to the policies of his own party. Phillips notes, for example, that between 1977 and 1988 the buying power of the average family among those in the top 1% increased by 49.8% from $270,000 to $404,566 while those in the bottom 80% experienced a decline in family earnings. Those in the bottom 10% experienced the steepest drop, 14.8%, as their income declined from $4,113 to $3,504 (Phillips, 1990, 17). Perhaps more revealing is the fact that the compensation of chief executive officers rose from twenty-nine times the income of the average manufacturing worker in 1979 to ninety-three times that average in 1988 (Phillips 1990, 179–80).

Integration of the U.S. economy into the global market has adversely affected those already struggling, unsuccessfully, to be winners in the marketplace at home. These developments have exacerbated polarization in the housing market in particular as well as in the economy generally. Emerging trends among lending institutions are most illustrative.

As in other industries, mortgage lenders (principally savings and loans and commercial banks) have experienced increasing foreign competition and declining profits in recent years. Like their counterparts in other industries, lenders claim they need greater flexibility to compete and, therefore, they have demanded deregulation primarily to permit investments previously closed to them under post-Depression era rules. The failure of many thrifts, the increase in mergers and acquisitions resulting in the concentration of financial institutions, the proliferation of interstate banking, and other forms of restructuring have dramatically altered lending patterns and practices.

One consequence, as described in the subsequent chapter, is a reduced commitment to mortgage lending by thrifts and more tenuous access to mortgage loans by central city residents. In turn, housing becomes more unaffordable, homelessness increases, and other housing-related problems are exacerbated (Meyerson 1986; Labaton 1991).

If housing choices are made by individual families, clearly those choices are shaped by the dynamics of institutional actors in the housing industry and the economy in general. Contrary to Nathan Glazer's characterization of housing as a free market involving millions of purchasers and hundreds of thousands of suppliers, and what has emerged as conventional housing wisdom, housing practice and policy cannot be understood simply in terms of a market of individual purchasers and suppliers. The production, distribution, and consumption of housing along with the related amenities is largely determined by powerful institutions and the unequal relations that prevail in the nation's political and economic institutions; relations that give rise to uneven spatial development of metropolitan areas and punish racial minorities, women, and others who are not real winners in the economic marketplace. Individual buyers and sellers do meet in the housing market, but that market is shaped and constrained by far more than personal taste and the economic capacity of homeseekers at that particular point in time. The process of capital accumulation, economic restructuring particularly as it plays out within local communities, and political activities by both public and private sector actors frame the context in which these decisions are made and they do so in a manner that fuels inequality and instability rather than equity and equilibrium.

Directions for Housing Policy

Developing more effective means to provide a decent home and a suitable living environment for every American family requires coming to terms with an array of structural and cultural forces shaping housing that are ignored or underconceptualized by mainstream ecological and neoclassical theories and most discussions of housing in scholarly and policy circles. Such research, at the same time, can inform broader questions of social inequality in American society. Emerging developments in housing and community development suggest new directions for policymakers and new roles for housing advocates in all sectors.

One key issue is the unfolding impact on housing of recent and proposed deregulation and the emerging restructuring of the housing industry. Federal law requires lending institutions to publicly disclose their mortgage lending activity by census tract as well as by race, gender, and income of mortgage loan applicants. In addition the federal Community Reinvestment Act (CRA—discussed in more detail in the following chapter) requires most lenders to assess and be responsive to the credit needs of the communities in which they operate including low- and moderate-income neighborhoods, though they must do so consistent with "safe and sound" lending practice (Squires 1992). The disclosure data enable regulators, community groups, and others to monitor mortgage lending activity and assess compliance with the CRA and other federal fair lending requirements. It is possible, therefore, to determine how effectively a given lender has met its CRA responsibilities and what the likely impact will be from a particular proposed merger, acquisition, or other form of institutional restructuring. (Lenders are required to apply to their respective federal financial regulatory agency to secure approval for such changes before they can take effect. Regulators can reject, and in response to pressure from community groups have denied or delayed consideration of, these applications until the lender agreed to improve its CRA performance.) Given the significant deregulation and restructuring that is likely to continue among financial institutions, expanding this kind of action research is critical at this point in time in order to generate additional reinvestment for currently disinvested communities. Such activity that has been taken under the auspices of the CRA within the past fifteen years has resulted in at least 300 reinvestment agreements with lenders in 70 cities calling for over $30 billion in urban reinvestment programs (Bradford 1992; Community Reinvestment Act Fact Sheet 1993, 3). Stronger law enforcement by federal financial regulatory agencies would likely lead to an expansion of credit availability in currently underserved areas.

Similarly, since the federal Fair Housing Act was strengthened research should be conducted to assess the impact of the changes in that statute. The number of findings of discrimination, the level of financial penalties that are invoked, and, most importantly, the impact on housing choice are issues that deserve close scrutiny in the coming years. More systematic testing of real estate agents, property insurers, and mortgage lenders would be most effective in identifying violations and securing remedies for victims. With two million instances of unlawful housing discrimination occurring each year and over half of all black and Hispanic homeseekers encountering discrimination in the housing market, stronger enforcement efforts are clearly warranted.

In recent years, debate over the value of housing integration has reemerged. On the one hand, it is argued that enforcing the nondiscrimination requirements of the law and assuring freedom of choice is the appropriate approach. If families, including nonwhite families, prefer a racially homogeneous neighborhood with all the amenities of a healthy neighorhood, that is their right. On the other hand, advocates of integration maintain that only by taking concrete steps to create and maintain stable integrated communities (e.g., providing financial incentives for pro-integrative moves, regulating the use of for-sale signs, marketing neighborhoods directly to underrepresented groups) will the forces that create the dual housing market and its adverse consequences for racial minorities be diminished and genuine freedom of choice be available (Leigh and McGhee 1986; DeMarco and Galster 1993). The historical reality is that racially segregated communities do experience highly unequal access to an array of public services and private benefits, including but in addition to physical shelter. Access to good housing and neighborhoods, unfortunately, often means access to predominantly white or integrated areas. Certainly exceptions to the rule exist, but it appears that the pursuit of stable integration and freedom of choice are mutually reinforcing rather than mutually exclusive options.

One promising response to racial segregation is represented by the Gatreaux program in Chicago which assists low-income black families in moving from public housing into private apartments throughout the six-county metropolitan area. The program began in 1976 as part of the remedy ordered by the federal courts after finding that the Chicago Housing Authority and HUD used unlawful discriminatory policies in locating public housing projects in that city. Over 4,700 families have subsequently been placed in private sector apartments. Among single female heads of households who have participated, more report holding jobs after they moved than before, particularly those who moved to the suburbs. Even after controlling on work history, education, training, age, and AFDC recipiency, suburban residents were more likely to have a job than their city counterparts (Rosenbaum and Popkin 1991; Gugliotta 1993, 1). The mothers also report greater satisfaction with their childrens' schools after the move. And while they experience greater unfriendliness among their neighbors than when they lived in the city, they also have more interracial friendships after relocating (Rosenbaum et al. 1986). While programs like the Gatreaux effort currently serve a small number of people, and more research on the work, school, and social experiences of parents and students is essential, results so far suggest at least one tool that should be used more widely to ameliorate racial segregation and its effects.

These findings do not suggest, however, that public housing is a universal failure. In fact many public housing projects do provide healthy living environments for low-income residents. In some cases, formerly crime-ridden, physically deteriorating, and unhealthy public housing units have been turned around, often by tenants themselves, into decent communities for the residents (Leavitt and Saegert 1990). Why some developments work while others fail remains largely an unanswered question.

Overseas, public housing is much more prevalent and carries far less of a stigma than is the case in the United States. One consequence is that the problems of affordability, homelessness, and inequality in consumption are not as severe (Van Vliet and Van Weesep 1990; Ball et al. 1988). More comparative work to determine how other countries have learned to use the public sector in partnership with private industry to provide housing for those not particularly successful in the economic marketplace generally would be informative for research, policy, and practice alike.

In recent years community development corporations and other nonprofit housing developers have built housing units for low- and moderate-income families. These efforts are often carried out in conjunction with local lenders, public housing and community development agencies, and private foundations, but clearly not in accordance with the privatistic ideology that has dominated housing throughout U.S. history. While accounting for a minuscule proportion of the nation's total housing stock, these efforts appear to be meeting a need that the conventional private market does not (Vidal 1990).

A related issue is the extent to which housing should be treated as a commodity to be produced, distributed, and consumed primarily via private markets as opposed to the extent to which housing should be viewed as a public right. This issue is embedded in a broader debate regarding the use value versus exchange value of urban space generally (Logan and Molotch 1987). At one level this may reflect conflicting values among consumers. Some home buyers are concerned primarily with the market (i.e., resale) value of their homes and certainly this is the case for real estate investors. But for many others increasing property values coupled with the declining buying power of their incomes are making adequate housing unaffordable or any housing unavailable at all. Consequently, housing is coming to be viewed by many as a right. If housing is a right, similar to education or perhaps as health care and health insurance are coming to be viewed, then what political and institutional mechanisms exist or can be created to implement this ideal? Proposals for a de-commodified approach to housing built around the concept of social ownership (where use value rather than exchange value would be the dominant force shaping the construction, financing, allocation, and utilization of housing) have been proposed by some housing advocates in recent years (Applebaum 1989; Zarembka 1990). As indicated above, specific programs have been experimented with at least on a small scale to complement, if not eventually replace, the private housing market. Perhaps these developments can eventually lead to elimination of the institutional constraints resulting in the contradictions noted by Stone regarding the relationship between the cost of housing and the price of labor as well as the business rationality that Harvey observes virtually dictates disinvestment of declining areas. More experimentation with such alternatives could lead to more housing opportunities for people whose needs are not being met by the current housing market. In addition to reshaping housing markets, these initiatives could also change popular conceptions of what properly falls within the domains of public and private life.

The common threads linking these somewhat diverse proposals all flow from critical tenets emerging from an institutional approach to housing and its challenge to privatism. They reflect an understanding of the central role of capital accumulation in the production, distribution, and consumption of housing and, therefore, suggest promising approaches to seemingly intractable problems given current institutional constraints. More specifically, they acknowledge the increasingly significant effects of economic restructuring on local urban development generally and on housing in particular, and, again, offer directions for overcoming the barriers these forces create for improving the nation's housing stock. Third they directly address the role of government, community organizations, and political action generally for both creating and, hopefully, resolving many of these problems. If this is not a disinterested agenda, it is one that can elucidate the dynamics of housing and, hopefully, options that are available for addressing one of the nation's most challenging social problems.

Still No Place Like Home

Edward C. Banfield argued almost twenty-five years ago that "the lower-class individual lives in the slum, which, to a greater or lesser extent, is an expression of his tastes and style of life" (Banfield 1968, 71). In drawing this conclusion Banfield ignored the wisdom of Louis Wirth who stated more than twenty years earlier:

> [I]t is important not to mistake the actual state of affairs for the underlying attitudes of people. Just because people live in the slums does not mean that they wish to live in them or that they hold housing in low esteem as a value. It may simply be that they are not able to help themselves, and if better housing were offered at a price they could meet, or if other items in their family budget were less demanding, housing would rise to a more important place. (Wirth 1947, 138)

The ability to understand and address housing problems turns on the capacity to recognize, and the willingness to address, the structural roots of these problems. The beginning point must be recognition of the role of housing within the broader political and economic structure of the United States. The centrality of the process of capital accumulation in housing, and housing's contribution to that process throughout the economy generally, the increasing integration of housing into the global economy and the consequences at the local level, the role of the public sector in facilitating these processes while attempting to legitimize the increasingly unequal outcomes, the privatistic ideological assumptions that have long driven housing, and the emerging conflicts surrounding the commodification of space provide a framework for understanding the contentious issues encompassing housing today.

The American dream of buying one's own home and moving up to a larger home and better neighborhood later on remains alive, despite the growing difficulty in achieving it. Homelessness, unaffordability, and denial of opportunity also remain, and in some respects are growing, realities in American life as well. Housing troubles are acutely felt by many individuals and their families. Yet these individual troubles are, in reality, social problems which need to be addressed as public issues (Mills 1959). Only by confronting these sociological realities will progress be made on housing issues. In turn, by focusing the sociological imagination on housing, much can also be learned about what drives and what divides American society.

4

Redlining and Community Reinvestment

Jesus Christ himself could not get a loan in Brooklyn.

A savings and loan president (Art 1987:1097)

Before anyone can contemplate buying a home, some means must be found to finance it. To get a business off the ground or to expand an existing enterprise, capital must be obtained. In the absence of rich relatives, this almost always means securing a loan from a financial institution. As is the case with employment and housing generally, housing and community development finance is provided on a highly uneven basis reflecting and reinforcing spatial and racial inequalities. Once again, global economic restructuring and the political response to those developments shape the provision of these services. Redlining is the charge diverse groups have leveled at financial institutions and reinvestment is the much sought-after remedy.

Despite an array of laws, regulations, and other administrative actions prohibiting racial discrimination in the provision of credit, racially discriminatory mortgage lending and disinvestment of older urban communities remain facts of city life. Yet these are facts around which there is significant struggle. True to the spirit of privatism most lenders as well as their regulatory agencies have generally denied the existence of widespread redlining or discrimination, claiming that each loan application is evaluated strictly on the basis of objective financial criteria. Since financial institutions make their money by making loans, it is argued that they have a self-interest that assures the elimination of any subjective practices that would undermine profitability. Recent research, however, has demonstrated systematic racial and geographic bias in lending and today even some within the industry are wavering in their denials.

Community organizations, civil right lawyers, some sympathetic public officials, and others who have long suspected redlining and racial discrimination are fighting back with some success. In fact, though not intended by the proponents of civil rights legislation, enforcement of fair housing and equal credit laws has been dominated by private actors. Such deferral of public authority to private—generally nonprofit—organizations, is at best a mixed blessing. Clearly, barriers to opportunities for life, liberty, and the pursuit of happiness could be reduced more effectively with a more aggressive public posture. Given fast developing changes in the structure of financial industries and the deregulatory thrust that continues among lawmakers, the significant achievements of private actors will need to be complemented by more effective public activity if reinvestment efforts are to continue and meaningful progress is to be made towards the goal of replacing the nation's ghettos with truly balanced and integrated living patterns.

When the Federal Fair Housing Act was passed in 1968 the U.S. Department of Housing and Urban Development (HUD) was designated as the chief law enforcement agency. The U.S. Department of Justice and several federal financial regulatory agencies also have critical law enforcement authority for fair housing and fair lending under the Fair Housing Act and subsequent legislation. Yet the vast majority of fair housing cases have been brought by private litigants and private litigation is responsible for the major decisions interpreting the 1968 act. The significance of private action is demonstrated by the fact that cities with private fair housing organizations generate a higher incidence of cases than communities not served by a fair housing group. Perhaps more important is the substantive development of the law resulting from private action. Privately initiated lawsuits resulted in rulings that the Fair Housing Act prohibited racial steering and exclusionary zoning; that discriminatory effect as well as intent can violate the law; that substantial damages for humiliation and other intangible injuries can be inferred from the fact of being victimized by discrimination; that discrimination against mortgage loan applicants due to neighborhood racial composition—redlining—is unlawful; and other interpretations that have provided substantial relief for victims of discriminatory housing and related practices (Schwemm 1988; Knapp 1987; Kushner 1988).

If private fair housing groups and litigants have been the principal

force for fair housing law enforcement, private community organizations have been the major force for compliance with the nation's fair
lending and community reinvestment laws. The key statute is the
Community Reinvestment Act enacted in 1977, which requires lenders
to be responsive to the credit needs of their entire service area, including low- and moderate-income neighborhoods. Virtually all the formal
rulings by the federal financial regulatory agencies charged with
enforcing this law resulted from challenges brought by private community groups (Art 1987, 1095). As indicated in the previous chapter,
reinvestment agreements totaling over $30 billion have been negoti-
ated with lenders by neighborhood organizations in over seventy
cities (Bradford 1992; Community Reinvestment Act Fact Sheet 1993,
3). "The true 'watchdogs' of the lending community with respect to
home finance discrimination matters have been private fair housing
groups and private citizens" (Dane and Henderson 1990, 223).

This chapter reviews the history of uneven lending practices,
focusing on the racial exclusion that has been a central dynamic of
mortgage lending and related housing industry practices. If private
groups are primarily responsible for recent enforcement activities, the
public sector long sanctioned racially discriminatory housing and
lending practices. Significant developments in fair lending law and
law enforcement are traced, followed by examples of how community-
based organizations have effectively utilized the leverage provided by
recent legislative initiatives. But there are serious limitations to private
action, particularly in light of current and proposed industry restructuring. In conclusion, recommendations are offered to ensure more
effective public and private enforcement of fair lending laws and to
nurture more comprehensive reinvestment in urban America.

Race and Mortgage Lending

Throughout most of this century intentional racial discrimination has
been an explicit requirement of housing finance and related housing
industry practices, with the full support of federal law. As indicated
earlier, both private sector and public sector actors have utilized race
as a criterion in making housing and housing-related services available in a manner that has segregated and destabilized neighborhoods
in cities across the country.

A central actor in the housing market is the appraisal industry.
Appraisers, upon whom lenders rely for determining property values,
long utilized racial composition of neighborhoods in their evaluations
(Schwemm 1993). If Frederick Babcock's observation half a century ago
that "race can result in very rapid decline" (Babcock 1932) appears

somewhat dated, the more recent 1975 edition of The Appraisal of Real Estate that "Economic obsolescence is caused by changes external to the property such as neighborhood infiltration of inharmonious groups" delivers the same message (Greene 1980, 10). Appraisers are often considered to be the eyes and ears of lending institutions. To this day, subjective assessments of neighborhoods frequently bias appraisal reports to the detriment of communities with large minority populations (Greene 1980, 7–10; Fair Lending Action Committee 1989, 5).

Similarly, realtors long practiced racial segregation contending that to do so was consistent with the highest ethical and professional standards of their industry. Not until 1950 did the National Association of Realtors remove from its code of ethics the warning that realtors should not bring into a community, "members of any race or nationality, or any individual whose presence will clearly be detrimental to property values in the neighborhood" (Judd 1984, 284). Again, as the Federal Housing Administration observed for many years, the two key groups in question were "Negroes and Mexicans" (Hoyt 1933, 315–16).

No innovation in housing policy has more effectively stimulated home ownership or suburbanization of metropolitan areas and the dual housing market associated with that decentralization than the federally insured mortgage. With the FHA insuring the majority of mortgages nationwide between the mid 1930s and early 1960s and less than 2 percent of these loans going to blacks, the agency directly subsidized suburban development and racial segregation of metropolitan areas. When the FHA shifted its policies in the 1960s and began doing most of its business in central cities, the principle effects were to line the pockets of unscrupulous lenders and real estate agents, destroy many central city neighborhoods, and deplete the savings of unwary first-time homebuyers.

Racial fears were often exploited, further destabilizing many urban neighborhoods. Real estate agents fostered the belief among many residents in older communities that their property values would decline if blacks moved in. In turn, the agents used a variety of tactics to encourage such white residents to sell, frequently at inflated prices initially. Black families would be enticed to buy, encouraging other white families to sell, often at subsequently depressed prices as the race card was played by real estate agents. Black families were then sold these homes, at great profit for the real estate agents as neighborhoods "tipped" from white to black. This process played out in several major cities during the 1960s, leaving behind dual housing markets that continue to plague these communities (Bradford 1990a; Jackson 1985).

Toward the end of the 1960s, federal law shifted dramatically, and the private housing industry began what was at least a verbalized about-face in its racial policies. With the Federal Fair Housing Act of

1968, the Equal Credit Opportunity Act of 1974, the Home Mortgage Disclosure Act of 1975, and most importantly the Community Reinvestment Act of 1977, along with several other federal, state, and local statutes, government policy shifted from a posture requiring segregation to one prohibiting it, at least in terms of the letter of the law. Not only is racial discrimination in housing and housing finance prohibited (along with other forms of discrimination that frequently serve as a cover for racial discrimination such as discrimination against families with young children), but affirmative marketing and other positive remedies are often required (G. Sloane 1983; M. Sloane 1983; Dane 1989; Schwemm 1989). During these years, real estate agents, appraisers, lenders, and other segments of the housing industry also officially expressed their support for the principles of fair housing and equal opportunity.

The Community Reinvestment Act of 1977 has been a particularly significant factor in shaping mortgage lending activity. By federal law, virtually all mortgage lenders now have an affirmative duty to address the credit needs of low-income neighborhoods. More importantly, the law created organizing opportunities for community groups to influence mortgage lending policies of private financial institutions. The CRA was enacted two years after the federal Home Mortgage Disclosure Act (HMDA) which required lenders to report the number and dollar volume of mortgage loans by census tract within metropolitan areas. As part of the savings and loan bailout plan, the Financial Institution Reform, Recovery, and Enforcement Act (FIRREA), beginning in 1990 HMDA also required disclosure of mortgage loan application and rejection rates by race, gender, and income. Despite limitations of HMDA, most notably the lack of information on credit rating, employment status, and condition of property (Wienk 1992; Galster 1991b), the information supplied by HMDA coupled with the requirements of CRA have altered the terms of the redlining debate.

Under the CRA federally regulated lenders "have a continuing and affirmative obligation to help meet the credit needs of the local communities in which they are chartered . . . consistent with safe and sound operation of such institutions." Lenders are required to prepare a CRA statement in which they map out their service areas and indicate the credit products they offer. In addition they are encouraged to ascertain the credit needs of those communities including low- and moderate-income areas, and indicate how they are meeting those needs. This statement, along with any comments received from the public pertaining to their CRA performance, must be available to the general public. Federal financial regulatory agencies are required to take lenders' CRA performances into account in evaluating applications for virtually any significant business transaction including applications for the establishment of a new branch bank, merger, acquisition, increased deposit insurance, or any related activity.

A critical component of the law is a provision allowing third parties—including community based-neighborhood organizations, nonprofit housing developers, and community development corporations—to file challenges to such applications in light of poor CRA records. Challenges can delay regulators' consideration of applications and even result in denials of the applications. Those delays can prove quite costly to the lenders. The costs provide the leverage for community groups. In order to expedite the processing of their applications, lenders often seek negotiations with those filing the challenge so that they will withdraw the challenge. With the information supplied by HMDA, community groups have negotiated several lucrative reinvestment agreements in recent years. (Specific examples are discussed below.) The CRA has dramatically altered the economic and political context in which mortgage lending occurs. Perhaps most importantly, few lenders today claim that their only concern is with the safety and soundness of their investments to be achieved solely by maximizing profitability for stockholders and depositors. Most lenders today acknowledge a responsibility to better serve diverse community credit needs (Art 1987). And many see no contradiction between community reinvestment and traditional business interests. As the former CRA officer and now vice president for Bank One in Milwaukee recently stated, "it's good business, you don't lose money doing CRA, it's the right thing to do" (Elverman 1990). (Not all lenders, of course, are convinced. In expressing his strong faith in the free market, a suburban Milwaukee lender stated that getting an outstanding CRA rating was "like being given the iron cross for service from the National Socialists Party" [Banker 1993, 23].)

FIRREA is also likely to make federal financial regulatory agencies more effective in encouraging reinvestment. As of 1 July 1990 regulators are required to publicly disclose the CRA ratings of all institutions reviewed after that date. Each institution is now placed in one of four rating categories: (1) outstanding record in meeting community credit needs, (2) satisfactory record, (3) needs to improve, and 4) substantial noncompliance in meeting community credit needs. In conducting their reviews regulators are required to examine a variety of lender practices including the geographic distribution of loans, marketing and types of credit available to communities, training programs to assure equal opportunity lending practices, and many other detailed characteristics of mortgage lending operations. Tighter regulatory oversight and publication of the overall CRA ratings should make the organizing efforts of community-based organizations even more effective.

Despite these favorable legal developments, the dual housing market and discriminatory effects of housing finance practices did not disappear in the sixties, seventies, or eighties. With black and Hispanic homeseekers still experiencing discrimination in over half their encounters with real estate agents (Turner et al. 1991, vi, 37) and HUD reporting 2 million instances of unlawful discrimination annually, racial inequality and racial segregation persist in the nation's housing markets (Schwemm 1989, 272). As indicated in the previous chapter, between 1970 and 1990 the extent of segregation between blacks and whites in major metropolitan areas remained virtually unchanged (Massey and Denton 1993). Despite the decentralization that has occurred in metropolitan populations in recent years, blacks are still more heavily concentrated near the city center than whites (Galster 1991a). Racial segmentation and stratification in housing remain defining traits of urban communities in the 1990s.

A persistent contributing factor is the nation's mortgage lending industry. Blacks continue to be rejected for mortgage loans twice as often as whites nationwide even among applicants within the same income groups (Dedman 1989; Canner and Smith 1991, 1992). As indicated previously, within metropolitan areas mortgage loans are more readily available in suburban and predominantly white neighborhoods than in central city and predominantly minority areas even after the effects of such factors as family income, quality of housing, residential turnover, and other factors associated with the credit worthiness of residents and security of their property are taken into consideration (Schafer and Ladd 1981; Shlay 1989; Bradbury et al. 1989; Squires and Velez 1987). And as researchers with the Boston Federal Reserve Bank found in its examination of over 3,000 applications with 131 lenders in that community, blacks are 60 percent more likely to be rejected than whites with identical credit records, debt histories, income, and other financial characteristics (Munnell et al. 1992). Intentional racial discrimination still exists, but in addition to instances of explicit discrimination and steering are the continuing effects of prior decades of mandated racial segregation and the adverse racial effects of contemporary institutional practices.

Several economic, social, and political factors account for continuing racial disparities in the mortgage market. Racial minorities do possess, on average, fewer economic resources than whites. And lending institutions enter into the homebuying process after other discriminatory acts may already have taken place by realtors, appraisers, property insurers and others (Wienk 1992). (Both historical and contemporary discrimination in employment and education, no doubt, contribute to a racial gap that even precedes entry into the housing market at any level. At the same time, housing discrimination, because of its affects on school choice and employment opportunities, makes the entire process a vicious circle.) Current policies and practices by financial institutions, nevertheless, contribute significantly to these racial disparities, and not simply by extending into the future the effects of historical discrimination within other institutions. Contemporary underwriting guidelines and the culture of many financial institutions coupled with lax law enforcement by regulatory agencies are major factors that perpetuate the adverse racial effects of home finance.

While explicit references to race may have disappeared from most underwriting manuals, underwriting guidelines still often adversely affect racial minorities. For example, many mortgage lenders will not make loans on low-valued properties, generally homes whose market value has been appraised at $25,000 to $35,000 or less. The reason is simply that since the costs of processing home mortgage loan applications vary little with the size of the loan, the profit margins on the smaller loans are frequently viewed as inadequate to justify the expenses. The solution for many lenders is to avoid the low end of the market. Such a policy, arguably, is predicated on no racial animosity. Yet it clearly has racial implications. Because racial minorities are more likely to live in lower-priced homes and in neighborhoods characterized by below-average home prices, this underwriting practice will disqualify a disproportionately high number of applications from racial minorities. To illustrate, in Milwaukee 21 percent of single-family dwellings were valued at $35,000 or less in 1988. Yet in those neighborhoods where racial minorities exceeded their city-wide representation of approximately 25 percent, 78 percent of single-family units were valued at this level (Squires et al. 1991). Similarly, some lenders have tighter underwriting restrictions for older homes, refuse to offer loans with a greater than 80 percent loan to value ratio thus requiring downpayments of 20 percent or more, offer no fixed rate loans with maturities over fifteen years, or refuse to offer FHA loans (Kohn 1993; Lawton 1993). Racial minorities tend to own older homes and to live in communities where the housing stock is generally older than in the balance of the metropolitan area. Due to their relatively lower income, they are more likely to participate in mortgage programs that allow for greater flexibility in downpayment requirements and longer amortization periods, and government-insured programs. Again, no racial discrimination may be intended, but one result of these practices is to exclude minorities more often than whites.

Subjective guidelines in many underwriting manuals can often be interpreted in ways that adversely affect racial minorities or any applicant that does not fit the norm for a given institution. For example, the Equitable Savings Bank in Milwaukee states that applicants should "have good character" and "a good reputation" and emphasizes that underwriters should use "*GOOD JUDGEMENT AND COMMON SENSE.*"

Underwriting guidelines of related institutions frequently discourage lenders from making particular loans. Requirements of private mortgage insurance companies and guidelines of secondary mortgage market institutions (e.g., Federal National Mortgage Association, Government National Mortgage Association, Federal Home Loan Mortgage Corporation) where lenders frequently sell their mortgages are often more restrictive than those of the originating lenders. One consequence is fewer loans to minority neighborhoods.

Even when the underwriting rules themselves are objective, the traditional culture of many lending institutions can shape the review process in a manner that adversely affects racial minorities. Most lenders prominently post signs indicating that they are equal opportunity lenders. But old ways die hard. Mortgage loan applications contain a wealth of information. While the information may be objective, evaluating the total package and making a final decision often entail subjective dimensions. If the underwriting standards are objective, inconsistent utilization of those standards frequently has racial effects. Overt racial prejudice clearly has not disappeared. Anecdotes are still reported from mortgage lending test audits where blacks are directed to a lender's mortgage corporation, whereas whites are encouraged to apply at the bank both testers initially contacted. In some cases blacks are steered to other lenders who make FHA loans, while whites are encouraged to apply for conventional financing. In other instances blacks are told it would be a lengthy process to determine if they qualify for a loan, while whites are assured it will take only a few minutes (Center for Community Change 1989; Lawton 1993). Some lenders are more likely to require credit checks for minority applicants than for nonminorities. Where substantial cash is available to the applicant for the downpayment, questions are more likely to be asked about how a minority family was able to accumulate the money, under the rarely stated but frequently suspected belief that in the case of minorities the money may have been derived from an unlawful source. In other cases, nonminority applications may be more closely scrutinized in order to determine if there are factors that may compensate for specific problems that might arise. For example, if the debt to income ratio is slightly higher than a lender's standards normally require, the lender might decide that a stable employment record, excellent credit record, or high downpayment might compensate for potential problems posed by the ratio. Lenders are more likely to look for such factors, to work with the applicant to secure a favorable outcome, in the case of nonminorities (Peterson 1990). The small number of minorities employed in lending institutions exacerbates these problems. In 1989 approximately 10 percent of officials and managers employed by banks and savings and loans were minority (U.S. Equal Employment Opportunity Commission 1989). And even when one out of ten loan officers is nonwhite, applications brought in by that person are frequently scrutinized more carefully than others, often adversely affecting minority homeseekers (Peterson 1990).

Unflattering racial stereotypes may have faded from the nation's financial institutions, but they have not disappeared. In a recent series of focus group interviews in twelve cities lenders were asked what distinguished black and white neighborhoods. As indicated in the previous chapter, several pointed to "pride of ownership" and "homeowner mentality" which they believed was more pervasive in white communities (ICF Incorporated 1991).

Lax law enforcement by federal fair housing and financial regulatory agencies is another critical factor in the perpetuation of racially discriminatory housing finance, leading one legal expert to conclude that "'Federal fair housing enforcement effort,' like such terms as 'military justice' and 'honest lawyer,' is an oxymoron" (Kushner 1988, 348). HUD's limited enforcement activity described earlier applies to its oversight activity related to financial institutions as well as real estate agents, property insurers, and other providers of housing-related services. The major federal financial regulatory agencies (i.e., Office of the Comptroller of the Currency, Federal Deposit Insurance Corporation, Federal Reserve System, Office of Thrift Supervision—formerly the Federal Home Loan Bank Board) have been similarly inactive in their enforcement responsibilities under the Community Reinvestment Act, Equal Credit Opportunity Act, Federal Fair Housing Act, and other rules.

One reason is their tendency to minimize prevailing fair lending problems while emphasizing "safety and soundness" matters in their regulatory activities. In 1989 a member of the board of governors of the Federal Reserve System told a subcommittee of the House Banking, Housing, and Urban Affairs Subcommittee, "Personally, I find it difficult to reconcile the notion that there is widespread racial discrimination in mortgage lending with the fact that bankers want to make loans. . . . I find the industry strongly committed as a matter of self-interest to make every sound loan possible" (LaWare 1990, 6). One year earlier the Comptroller of the Currency stated "banks historically have helped to meet local community credit needs, consistent with safety and soundness requirements, and they continue to do so" (Dane 1990, 262).

At least in part because of these attitudes, the regulatory agencies have not utilized enforcement tools that have proven so effective in private litigation. Minimal use of statistical analysis, testing, and the effects test (defined by the FDIC as "conduct which has a disproportionate adverse impact on a protected group or which has the effect of perpetuating segregated housing . . . regardless of intent" [Seidman

1990, 69]) are some of those tools that have not been adequately employed by HUD, Justice, and financial regulatory agencies (Dane 1990; Schwemm 1990). In fact, it was only following a lawsuit (*Urban League et al. v. Comptroller of the Currency et al.*, U.S. District Court for the District of Columbia, C.A. No. 76–0718) by a coalition of civil rights groups that the financial regulatory agencies even promulgated regulations to enforce the Community Reinvestment Act, the Fair Housing Act, the Equal Credit Opportunity Act, and other federal fair lending rules (Dane 1990, 261).

There is evidence that some federal agencies may become more aggressive in the future. At a 1992 conference on housing discrimination research sponsored by the Federal National Mortgage Association (Fannie Mae), the chairman and chief executive office of the association concluded, "The papers presented today make clear that discrimination continues to limit access to housing and mortgage credit for many citizens. The challenge now facing the housing community is to fashion solutions that remedy these disturbing findings" (Fannie Mae 1992). HUD recently sponsored a nationwide testing program in mortgage lending. In 1992 the U.S. Department of Justice settled the first pattern and practice lawsuit brought by the federal government against a mortgage lender resulting in $1 million for forty-eight black applicants rejected by the bank and several changes in its underwriting, marketing, and employment practices (U.S. Department of Justice 1992). Settlements have since been reached with three other lenders and more investigations are pending. The Office of the Comptroller of the Currency which regulates national banks announced in May 1993 that by the end of the year it would develop a pilot program to use testers as part of its efforts to explore two related issues: (1) whether loan applicants with the same qualifications achieve the same results regardless of race or national origin, and (2) whether banks provide the same levels of assistance to minority and nonminority applicants during the loan process (Comptroller of the Currency 1993). And late in 1993 the Clinton Administration proposed new CRA regulations calling for examiners to focus more directly on lending performance while providing stiffer penalties for lenders with poor re-investment records.

Yet enforcement of fair housing and fair lending rules has been spotty at best. The financial regulatory agencies responsible for compliance with the CRA have been the least sympathetic to equal opportunity matters among those with fair lending enforcement authority. The CRA has proven to be a valuable resource. However, as one observer noted, "the driving force behind the successful implementation of the CRA's purposes has been activist community organizations" (Dane 1990, 262).

The focus of most activity has been on mortgage lending. But there is also evidence that racial minorities have encountered discrimination in efforts to secure commercial and other types of business loans, that black-owned businesses receive smaller loans than white-owned businesses with comparable financial characteristics, and that central cities have experienced redlining in these credit areas as well (Updegrave 1989; Bates 1989, 1991). No data set comparable to HMDA is publicly available to allow for analysis of business lending similar to the research that has been conducted on mortgage loans. Yet it is evident that successful community reinvestment requires access to business as well as home loans. If HMDA, CRA and related laws pertaining to fair lending were motivated primarily by concerns over discrimination in mortgage lending, they have also been used to stimulate commercial and business loans in distressed communities.

The Reality of Reinvestment

The existence of laws, alone, of course, is rarely sufficient to significantly alter behavior. But as part of a diversified tool kit, CRA has proven critical in successful efforts to secure new dollars for home financing and community reinvestment generally for residents of low- and moderate-income areas, many of which have large minority populations, in cities throughout the country. Working with knowledgeable reporters in local print and electronic media, supportive academic researchers, aggressive labor and church groups, and sympathetic local and state officials, many community-based organizations have utilized the information available through HMDA and leverage provided by CRA to stimulate reinvestment activities in dozens of cities. The following stories are illustrative.

Chicago

The city of Chicago has perhaps the longest history of effective grass-roots community organizing. Prior to HMDA and CRA community groups used a variety of Alinsky-style direct action tactics to bring banks to the negotiating table. These included picket lines, disruption of normal business by dropping hundreds of pennies on the floors of bank lobbies at peak hours, and flooding bank offices with people who opened and closed accounts for $1. One Chicago community group, the Organization of the NorthEast, negotiated a written reinvestment agreement with the Bank of Chicago in 1974, three years before the CRA was enacted, following a citizen-organized direct action campaign against the bank.

Community-based organizations in that city led the political fights to secure passage of HMDA and CRA, and Chicago area community organizations were among the first to utilize these laws subsequent to their passage. In 1984 the Community Reinvestment Alliance, a coalition of more than thirty community organizations, negotiated agreements totaling $173 million over five years with three major banks in that city; First Chicago, Harris Bank, and Northern Trust. In 1988 and 1989 all three announced extensions of these agreements for an additional five-year commitment of $200 million. (Agreements were also subsequently signed with several smaller community banks and community groups throughout the city.) The agreements, known as the Neighborhood Lending Program, called for specific types of loans, for particular dollar amounts in designated areas. This program created new dollars for mortgages, home improvement loans, home equity loans, business and commercial loans, mixed-use real estate financing, and other types of housing and commercial lending. Community groups play central roles in designing the loan programs, packaging the loans, and monitoring the agreements. Review boards consisting of community and banking members have been established to provide accountability and oversee implementation of the agreements. To strengthen the capacity of the community members of these partnerships, the three banks have committed up to $3 million in direct grants from their foundations for those involved in housing and business development. Many of the elements of the Chicago programs have served as role models nationwide and have been incorporated in agreements signed in many other cities (Bradford 1990b; National Council for Urban Economic Development undated; Pogge 1992).

Boston

A study for the Federal Reserve Bank of Boston triggered a major reinvestment commitment by that city's ten largest banks (Bradbury et al. 1989). In their research for the Federal Reserve three economists analyzed mortgage lending patterns between 1982 and 1987 and found a substantial disparity in lending activity between predominantly black and predominantly white neighborhoods. This gap persisted after various nonracial characteristics that could account for differences in lending across neighborhoods are taken into consideration. The key finding was that the ratio of mortgage loans to potentially mortgageable housing was 24 percent higher in white areas after controlling on such factors as family income and wealth, housing value and age, vacancy rates, new housing construction, and other economic and demographic factors. Shortly after the press releases were issued announcing the findings of this study, six community organizations formed the

Community Investment Coalition. After months of public pressure and private negotiations, assisted with the aggressive support of Mayor Raymond Flynn, Boston's ten largest banks and the community coalition announced a $400 million five-year lending program. The program includes increased dollars for mortgage loans (some at below market rates) in inner city communities, funds for new construction of affordable housing, new branch banks, and improved services for inner city residents including cashing of welfare and social security checks, additional automatic teller machines, expanded services, and other provisions for reinvestment (Campen 1990a; Dreier 1990).

Atlanta

A Pulitzer prize winning series of newspaper articles, "The Color of Money," (Dedman 1988) stimulated a $65 million lending agreement among several banks in Atlanta. With the assistance of Calvin Bradford of Community Reinvestment Associates and Charles Finn with the Hubert Humphrey Institute at the University of Minnesota, reporter Bill Dedman found that whites received five times as many home loans as blacks with similar incomes. The *Atlanta Journal/Constitution* series stimulated widespread debate in that city. State banking regulators called for more stringent rules governing lending. The Fulton County Commission unanimously approved a fair housing ordinance. And a coalition of neighborhood groups, the Atlanta Community Reinvestment Alliance, filed a series of CRA challenges. While refuting accusations of racism, the city's major lenders agreed to a reinvestment program that included the creation of a $20 million loan pool by nine lenders targeted to working class neighborhoods, a $25 million commitment for low-interest loans for home purchase and home improvement for families with incomes below $35,000 in any community by Citizens and Southern Bank, a similar $10 million commitment from First Atlanta Bank, and a $10 million program with low-interest loans in targeted areas from Trust Company Bank.

Detroit

In Detroit a 1988 newspaper series, "The Race for Money," also played a major role in launching a $2.9 billion lending program in that city. *Detroit Free Press* reporter David Everett led an investigation, again with the help of Bradford and Finn, which found that local lenders were not as heavily involved in major local development projects as were other lenders in major cities nationwide, Detroit lenders had low participation in government loan programs designed to help individuals and businesses experiencing difficulty securing conventional loans, and mortgage loan patterns were racially biased favoring white homeowners. The Ad Hoc Coalition for Fair Banking Practices including an array of housing groups, the United Auto Workers, the NAACP, churches, New Detroit Inc. (a powerful civic organization including leaders with Detroit's business, political, and cultural institutions) and others was formed to negotiate more support from local lenders. Aggressive implementation of a state community reinvestment act by Eugene Kuthy, Commissioner of the Michigan Financial Institutions Bureau from 1983 to 1990, also served as a critical catalyst. When Kuthy denied an application by Comerica Inc., the second largest banking company in Michigan, to purchase a Texas bank because of a poor CRA record, the negotiations began. Altogether seven institutions—Comerica, First America Bank of Southeast Michigan, Manufacturers National Bank, Michigan National Bank, First Federal of Michigan, Standard Federal Bank, and National Bank of Detroit—agreed to a total of $2.9 billion over three years in a combination of housing, business, and consumer loans. It is estimated that this will amount to an increase of $350 million in new loans that otherwise would not have been made with at least $70 million for new home mortgage loans. Perhaps more importantly, what began as a most contentious adversarial process has evolved into a collaborative effort to reinvest in Detroit (Everett 1992).

Pittsburgh

In Pittsburgh a coalition of twenty-three community development corporations utilized leverage provided by the CRA to negotiate a $109 million five-year neighborhood reinvestment agreement with Union National Bank (UNB). The Pittsburgh Community Reinvestment Group (PCRG) secured financing for conventional home mortgages, commercial real estate, and minority business development. In addition the bank agreed to implement CRA training for its personnel, improved branch banking services, and affirmative action hiring. Direct grants are also provided to fund operating costs of community development corporations in Pittsburgh. Implementation of the UNB agreement was followed by successful negotiations with several additional banks and savings and loans in that community (Metzger 1990).

Milwaukee

Several waves of organizing have generated commitments from over a dozen lenders in Milwaukee. There is evidence that more commitments will soon be forthcoming.

A coalition of community-based organizations in Milwaukee nego-tiated $50 million in lending agreements with that city's third largest bank in 1986 (Marine Corporation later changed to Bank One when Marine was taken over by Banc One Corporation) and largest savings and loan (First Financial) in 1989. In addition to a variety of loan and banking service commitments the bank agreed to open a new inner city branch and the thrift agreed to an affirmative action hiring plan.

The 1989 *Atlanta Journal/Constitution* (Dedman 1989) news story generated additional interest when it reported that Milwaukee had the highest racial disparity in mortgage loan rejection rates of any city nationwide. (Blacks were rejected four times as often as whites in Mil-waukee compared to a two-to-one ratio nationwide.) Milwaukee's Democratic Mayor and the state's Republican governor created a Fair Lending Action Committee (FLAC) consisting of lenders, regulators, civil rights groups, city officials, and other community organizations to formulate a plan to increase lending to racial minorities. A set of twenty-eight recommendations was developed, including specific numerical goals for residential, commercial real estate, and business loans for racial minorities in the Milwaukee metropolitan area. While implementation of these recommendations has proceeded slowly, FLAC has helped spur related reinvestment efforts. In part because of disappointment in the efficacy of FLAC, in 1990 a Fair Lending Coali-tion (initially called the Fair Lending Project) was formed under which a variety of neighborhood associations, civil rights organizations, churches, labor unions, faculty and graduate students at a local uni-versity, and others began meeting with individual lenders to negotiate lending programs. With the assistance of the Fair Lending Coalition Norwest Bank launched a $25 million program including residential and commercial lending objectives, feasibility study for a new inner city branch, and outreach efforts to increase minority employment. Equitable Savings Bank agreed to a $7 million program in addition to several new marketing tactics. For example, brochures describing bank products will be distributed in several languages including Spanish, Laotian, and Hmong. And the bank will work with five central city employers to assist their employees in purchasing homes near their place of work (Glabere 1992). Five other formal agreements have been negotiated totaling over $40 million in commitments for central city mortgage and business loans, an additional branch bank, and addi-tional changes in marketing and employment practices (Norman 1992, 1993a; *The Business Journal* 1993; copies of the original agreements are available in author's files). Other lenders on their own initiative have contacted the coalition to develop similar reinvestment programs. While some lenders expressed concern with some tactics of the Fair Lending Coalition, clearly its aggressive approach has been critical to its success. As the headline of an editorial by the local business news-paper read, "'Confrontational' style is lending project's strength" (*The Business Journal* 1992, 4).

In June of 1993 Milwaukee Inner City Congregations Allied for Hope (MICAH, a coalition of thirty-five city churches) secured five-year commitments from eight institutions totaling $284 million in resi-dential and business loans for neighborhoods served by these churches. These lenders also signed pledges to follow various princi-ples of fairness and equity in their dealings with the community. The MICAH area is about fifty percent larger than the inner city neighbor-hoods targetted by the Fair Lending Coalition, so these commitments will reach more diverse segments of Milwaukee. There is some ques-tion whether these commitments would result in any additional lend-ing in the inner city, at least for some of the participating lenders. If less targeted, and if less ambitious than it appears, these commitments may still serve the broader concern with reinvestment, and more lenders indicated the likelihood that they will be signing off on the principles and making specific loan dollar commitments (Norman 1993b).

Other Communities

There are many other examples where community groups have used similar tactics to achieve similar results. In Cincinnati, Communities United for Action secured a $113 million five-year agreement with the four major banks in that city (Braykovich 1990). In Dallas, ACORN negotiated an agreement with Texas Commerce Bank for $2.5 million in mortgage and home improvement loans. ACORN and the Innercity Development Corporation then negotiated a $25 million five-year agreement with RepublicBank subsequently taken over by North Car-olina National Bank, which has agreed to honor the commitment. In Dayton, the city government and seven participating banks announced a Neighborhood Lending Program with a goal of investing $10 million in housing in selected city neighborhoods. In Denver ACORN negotiated a three-year $5.4 million program with United Bank of Denver for residential lending. Two CRA agreements in Wash-ington, D.C. culminated in five-year lending commitments; $10 million by United Virginia Bankshares (which subsequently changed its name to Crestar) and $40 million by Riggs National Bank. Both programs focus on business and economic development (National Council for Urban Economic Development undated).

Two statewide reinvestment campaigns, one on the East Coast and one on the West Coast, have resulted in major reinvestment commit-ments. In Florida the state's five largest bank holding companies responded to a request from Legal Services with a statewide lending agreement. Though no dollar amounts were specified, Legal Services estimates that the five-year programs combined will generate $100 million per year in credit, investments, and contributions to affordable housing initiatives and minority businesses. In California organizing on reinvestment issues goes back at least to the 1970s. By the late 1980s a statewide coalition of community based advocacy groups, local public officials, and consultant organizations negotiated agreements with California lenders totaling over $350 million. Continued efforts by neighborhood groups, regulators, local officials, and industry groups have resulted in more sophisticated monitoring by reinvestment advocates, a range of city programs and a ten-year $8 billion commitment by three major banks: Bank of America, Security Pacific, and Wells Fargo (National Council for Urban Economic Development undated; Rosen 1992). Reinvestment is occuring, albeit in varying degrees, in communities throughout the United States.

Public Entrepreneurship

Sympathetic public officials have assisted many CRA initiatives. In Boston, for example, Mayor Raymond Flynn took an active leadership role that led directly to that city's $400 million agreement. In Milwaukee, Mayor John Norquist took the lead in forming the Fair Lending Action Committee and the city has provided financial support for the Fair Lending Coalition. More entrepreneurial initiatives to stimulate reinvestment have been launched by these and many other local officials.

Boston and Milwaukee are two of at least twelve cities and Massachusetts is one of at least fourteen states that have recently implemented linked deposit programs under which depositories of public funds are required to have a good community reinvestment record. At the end of 1989 state and local government deposits totaled $73 billion, over 2 percent of all deposits held by depository institutions (Campen 1990b). The criteria vary among the different linked deposit programs. They include a commitment to mortgage lending in low- and moderate-income areas, loans to minority- and female-owned businesses, affirmative action and equal opportunity in employment, ongoing communication with community groups to assess credit needs, participation in publicly sponsored low- and moderate-income lending programs, and contributions to community philanthropic activities. Given lenders' concerns with public relations (and their desires to achieve a good CRA rating) simply publicizing relative reinvestment performances of local lenders can be beneficial.

A related and potentially more effective dimension of linked deposit programs occurs when other institutions like union pension funds, religious organizations, nonprofit agencies, and individual savers follow their city's lead (or sometimes precede city action) by depositing their funds with more responsive lenders. These institutions in fact control far more deposits than do state and local governments. Accurate and widely publicized reporting of lender reinvestment records by the public sector can significantly strengthen these activities. While no systematic evidence has been compiled on the extent of these efforts, such "greenlining" campaigns have substantially expanded the pool of capital for reinvestment.

A variety of approaches have been utilized in recent years to increase the availability of housing and community development finance with CRA organizing campaigns being perhaps the most notable. Most are too recent to permit systematic evaluation. One conclusion that can be drawn, however, is that these local community-based efforts would be strengthened considerably by a more aggressive approach on the part of federal regulatory agencies.

The Future of Fair Lending and Community Reinvestment

Successful local reinvestment efforts offer promise for the future. But that future is clouded by recent trends towards centralization, globalization and homogenization of the nation's financial industries and the push for deregulation, justified by many within these institutions as essential for meeting foreign competition and maximizing the efficiency with which capital is invested. With a strong federal CRA enforcement effort, however, such restructuring may offer even greater opportunities for reinvestment.

As indicated in the previous chapter financial institutions have responded to increasing foreign competition and declining profitability in part with increasing merger activity, acquisitions, and concentration generally, nurtured by deregulation. One concrete result of these developments has been a declining number of lenders—from 20,000 in the early 1970s to 16,000 in 1990 (Bradford and Cincotta 1992)—and increasing concentration among those remaining competitors. Lenders claim they need more flexibility if they are going to be able to compete in the new world market. Deregulation—permitting thrifts and commercial banks to enter financial services (e.g., commercial real estate development for thrifts and insurance for commercial banks) and geographic locations (via expansion of interstate and international banking) previously closed to them under the post-Depression financial industry regulatory structure that was established and held firm through the early 1980s—has been demanded and, in large part, granted, though large commercial banks are seeking even greater regulatory relief (Meyerson 1986; Labaton 1991). The recent merger of two of the nation's ten largest banks, Chemical Bank and Manufacturers Hanover Trust, is both a symbolic and substantive indication of recent developments within financial institutions. Prior to the merger Chemical Bank, with $72.5 billion in assets, was the nation's seventh largest bank. Manufacturer's Hanover Trust, with $64.8 billion, was the eighth largest. After the merger, with $137.3 billion, the newly formed bank was the nation's second largest (Quint 1991).

Deregulation, concentration, and globalization of financial institutions raises serious questions about the availability of funds to finance home ownership, particularly for low-income families, as the ties between particular institutions and communities are weakened. When lenders who previously devoted substantial resources for home mortgages offer new products and enter new markets, housing investment becomes one of several options that must compete with virtually all other types of investment. If suburban shopping malls in San Diego or steel production in Seoul become more attractive investments for financial institutions than housing, then that is where capital will flow. The movement of capital through various circuits is expedited along with the instability it breeds at the neighborhood level, particularly in already depressed urban communities. In recent years savings and loans have indeed diversified out of housing as the percentage of thrift investments in residential real estate declined from 80 percent in 1978 to 54 percent in 1988 (*Savings Institutions Sourcebook* 1990, 30). And, as many savings and loans in the United States have demonstrated, deregulation can result in lenders entering markets unwisely leading to the bankruptcy of their institutions (Pizzo et al. 1989). In general, concentration of financial institutions tends to result in increasing costs for customers (Brown 1991). One direct consequence is the increasing unaffordability of housing, rising homelessness, and related problems discussed earlier.

At least at the present time, however, applications for mergers, acquisitions, and other changes in business operations must be approved by federal financial regulatory agencies that are charged by law to consider CRA performance in each application. Restructuring of U.S. financial institutions can present opportunities to enhance fair lending and reinvestment, if key regulatory agencies take a more aggressive approach to their CRA responsibilities.

Several specific steps could be taken to immediately improve the effectiveness of fair lending law enforcement. Other more ambitious steps could be taken over a longer period of time, but would assure the permanence of the incremental gains that are being made.

First, pre-purchase counseling could be expanded particularly for the benefit of first-time buyers to help more renters become homeowners and to assure that they purchase homes they can afford to maintain. Congress could authorize increased funding for community-based nonprofit organizations currently providing these services and counseling could be included as an activity that would be considered by financial regulatory agencies in determining CRA ratings of lenders and evaluating challenges to their performance (Bradford 1990a, 5).

Law enforcement agencies could monitor more aggressively current lending policies and practices by conducting their own analyses of HMDA and other data that they collect. Rather than simply responding to complaints, applications, or CRA challenges, the agencies could identify potential problem areas through statistical analyses. Only within the past two or three years have financial regulatory agencies begun to make use of such tools and to complement their complaint investigations with agency-initiated investigations into these issues (Dane 1991, 120–21; Chud and Bonnette 1993; Goldstein 1993). While the use of statistics alone may not prove unlawful discrimination, such studies can help agencies target scarce law enforcement resources.

Far more comprehensive and effective use could be made of testing for mortgage lending bias by law enforcement agencies. Statistical analyses of mortgage lending patterns can be particularly useful in determining where testing would be most productively utilized. Agencies themselves could perform the tests and increased funds could be made available to those private agencies that have demonstrated the capacity to use this tool (Smith 1990, 268–70; Smith and Cloud 1993; Fishbein 1990, 176–77; Lawton 1993; Leeds 1993; Wallace et al. 1985). Over the past two years HUD has provided increasing funding for private fair housing groups to conduct testing programs, including tests of mortgage lenders. (The U.S. Equal Employment Opportunity Commission now accepts charges based on testing evidence and has issued guidelines on their use, testifying to the utility of testing as an enforcement tool in the area of equal employment opportunity [U.S. Equal Employment Opportunity Commission 1990].) Again, however, federal financial regulatory agencies have been slow to follow this lead (Relman 1991, 111–12; Dane 1991, 123–24). Testing could be an effective instrument for public officials in monitoring lending patterns, assessing individual complaints, documenting unlawful lending practices, and assuring compliance with court orders, regulatory agency rulings, and court decrees (The Rockefeller Foundation and The Urban Institute 1991).

Coupled with the use of statistics and testing would be greater use of the effects test in law enforcement activities. Underwriting rules that adversely affect minority or low-income mortgage loan applicants such as minimum loan amounts, closing costs or interest rates tied to size of loan, or use of age alone as a criterion could be prohibited (Dane 1989, 265; Relman 1991, 117).

One extremely simple step would be to provide routine, mandatory disclosure of appraisal reports for buyers and their brokers. Given the central role of the appraisal in underwriting decisions and the fact that mortgage applicants pay for this service, public disclosure would be a logical step. Knowing that these reports would be disclosed, lenders would take greater care in assuring the accuracy of reports on which they base adverse decisions and appraisers would likely provide more objective and reliable information (Fishbein 1990a, 1990b).

A valuable additional area of disclosure would be commercial loans. Availability of mortgage loans, in the absence of adequate credit for commercial businesses, would only temporarily delay disinvestment in both business and home lending. Disclosure of business loans, and use of that data in enforcement activities, would facilitate many current reinvestment efforts.

CRA requirements could be applied to other types of financial institutions including insurers, finance companies, mutual funds, mortgage banks and brokerage firms, and others (Campen 1993). In June 1993 the Treasury Department announced that it would launch a study to assess whether or not money market funds, consumer financing companies, and automobile finance companies should be required to comply with the CRA. Frank N. Newman, Under Secretary for Domestic Finance observed that as nonbanking institutions like these grow, in part by attracting funds that previously would have been deposited with commercial banks or thrifts, they become increasingly significant actors in the larger economy and, therefore, it is appropriate to determine what their community reinvestment responsibilities ought to be (Greenhouse 1993). Such financial institutions could bring additional resources to the reinvestment effort and appropriate regulatory action would encourage movement in that direction.

Employment practices by mortgage lenders and other financial institutions could be brought under the auspices of CRA. Existence, (or nonexistence) of effective affirmative action plans could be incorporated as one of the criteria on which CRA ratings and reviews of CRA challenges would be considered. Lenders participating in federal insurance programs could be viewed and treated similar to federal contractors and, therefore, required to meet the affirmative action and equal employment opportunity responsibilities that contractors must meet under Executive Order 11246.

Penalties for violation of fair lending laws could be strengthened. One sanction regulatory agencies could invoke would be to cancel or increase the cost of federal depository insurance for any lender who violated fair lending or community reinvestment laws (Bradford 1990a, 3–4). Such a tool could be used flexibly to assure that the punishment was commensurate with the violation. Criminal laws could be enacted that would result in forfeiture of property sold or financed in violation of fair housing or fair lending laws and revocation of licenses of realtors, lenders, and others who facilitate such transactions (Zarembka 1990, 117–18).

Other longer-term policies should be considered. Greater effectiveness and efficiencies would be obtained by combining all fair lending and community reinvestment rules into one statute administered by one agency (Dane and Henderson 1990, 224–28). While lending expertise would obviously be required, the focus of the agency's work should be civil rights law enforcement. Among those who currently have civil rights compliance responsibilities in these areas, HUD might be the appropriate department to house such a consolidated law enforcement effort.

To dramatically increase the supply of credit for low-income and other depressed neighborhoods, a simple, yet comprehensive, and probably politically unfeasible approach in the current climate, would be the creation of publicly funded nonprofit housing banks. Without the pressure to generate profits, interest rates sufficient to cover the costs of administration and the risk of bad loans could be reduced, to as low as two or three percent according to some experts (Zarembka 1991). Savings over the life of a loan would be significant. For example, a twenty-five-year $40,000 loan at 12 percent would cost $86,300 over the life of the loan compared with $10,860 at 2 percent. Capitalization for such banks could come from the elimination of mortgage interest and real estate tax deductions for wealthy homeowners, deposits from some tax-exempt organizations in return for their exemption, and high capital gains taxes on short-term speculative real estate transactions. Political resistance would be expected from several quarters. But as the costs of the savings and loan bailout increase and the likelihood of a bank bailout looms larger, while increasing numbers of families are priced out of homeownership, that resistance might quickly fade. If such a proposal is not feasible today, debate over President Clinton's call for a series of development banks may lead to a discussion along these lines within a few years.

These federal initiatives would complement the many local and state efforts, both public and private, that have grown in recent years. And expansion of these experiments would feed back into further recommendations for federal initiatives, thus strengthening fair lending and reinvestment activities at all levels nationwide.

It is doubtful that current dependence on private initiatives can lead to adequate law enforcement, or that such privatization is good for the economy, except perhaps for a few special interests in the very short run. The limits on private civil rights law enforcement generally or fair lending in particular are severe. Many victims do not even know that they in fact are being victimized. Many who are aware of the injustice they suffer do not have the funds to take legal action, or access to a fair housing center who can act for them. Among those with the means, many simply do not have the time or energy to invest in a lawsuit (Schwemm 1988, 379–81). Private action will always be a vital part of fair lending and reinvestment law enforcement. It is necessary, but not sufficient.

Many of these recommendations would meet with at least initial resistance, particularly from representatives of the lending industry. CRA and related fair lending activities have often been initiated amidst great conflict frequently generating even more personal and institutional antagonism in the early stages. Yet those animosities have often been overcome by community organizers and lenders who came to perceive common interests. Many lenders who have worked with community organizations and fair housing groups have found those relationships quite productive, eventually recognizing no conflict between their business interests and the community needs. Fair lending, community reinvestment, and balanced development of metropolitan areas are in the long term interests of most if not all parties to these debates. The health of the nation's cities depends on achieving these goals.

A Cautionary Note on Partnerships

Many partnerships that have emerged through the reinvestment movement have proven effective. A critical reason for that success is the fact that community-based organizations have nurtured many allies. A second key has been the development of several tools— including new federal laws—that have enabled them to negotiate on a more level playing field than was the case just a few years ago. Laws like the federal Fair Housing Act, HMDA, and CRA; cooperative elected officials at all levels of government; sympathetic news reporters; and supportive academics have all helped community groups confront lending institutions.

Unfortunately, the optimism with which many observers point to the role of public-private partnerships for urban redevelopment generally, in part because of successful CRA campaigns, has proven to be misplaced. The basic flaw in both the concept and actual practice of public-private partnerships in the broader economic development arena is the fundamentally unequal relationship that still characterizes these efforts, as the following chapter will show.

5

Partnership and the Pursuit of the Private City: Urban Redevelopment in the United States

> . . . two hundred and sixty-eight years of laissez-faire economics had left the city in a hell of a mess.
>
> Joseph S. Clark, Jr., mayor of Philadelphia,
> 1952–1956 (Warner 1987: xi)

Public-private partnerships have become the rallying cry for economic development professionals throughout the United States (Porter 1989; Davis 1986). As federal revenues for economic development, social service, and other urban programs diminish such partnerships are increasingly looked to as the key for urban revitalization (Peterson and Lewis 1986). These partnerships take many forms. Formal organizations of executives from leading businesses have been established which work directly with public officials. In some cases public officials as well as representatives from various community organizations are also members, as was the case with many of the reinvestment partnerships discussed in the previous chapter. Some partnerships have persisted for decades working on an array of issues while others are ad hoc arrangements that focus on a particular time-limited project. Direct subsidies from public agencies to private firms have been described as public-private partnerships. If economic development has emerged as a major function of local government, public-private partnerships are increasingly viewed as the critical tool.

The concept of partnership is widely perceived to be an innovative approach that is timely in an age of austerity. In fact "public-private partnership" is little more than a new label for a longstanding relationship between the public and private sectors. Growth has been the constant, central objective of that relationship, though in recent years subsidization of dramatic economic restructuring has become a complementary concern. While that relationship has evolved throughout U.S. history, it has long been shaped by the ideology of privatism which has dominated urban redevelopment from colonial America through the so-called postindustrial era. Even more than in the areas of employment and housing, privatism has infused the logic behind and the practice of local redevelopment. Public-private partnerships simply represent the most recent embodiment of this long dominant belief.

The central tenet of privatism, as indicated in previous chapters, is the belief in the supremacy of the private sector and market forces in nurturing development with the public sector as a junior partner whose principle obligation is to facilitate private capital accumulation. Individual material acquisitiveness is explicitly avowed, but that selfishness is justified by the public benefits that are assumed to flow from the dynamics of such relations.

One need look no further than the roadways, canals, and railroads of the eighteenth and nineteenth centuries to see the early concrete manifestations of large scale public subsidization of private economic activity and the hierarchical relationship between the public and private sectors (Langton 1983; Krumholz 1984). These relationships crystallized in the urban renewal days of the fifties and sixties and in the widely celebrated partnerships of the eighties. Structural changes in the political economy of cities, regions, and nations over time have altered the configuration of specific public-private partnerships, but not the fundamental relationship between the public and private sectors. These structural changes have, however, influenced the spatial development of cities and exacerbated the social problems of urban America.

Contemporary partnerships reflect a traditional, historical relationship between the public and private sectors. While in recent years they have taken some new forms and are justified by some additional arguments, the continuity they represent far outweighs the innovation. Within the postwar years, and particularly within the past two decades, formal organizations have been established that are designed to include leadership from business and industry along with representation from local government, and frequently including members from cultural, educational, and other social institutions. In their current formulations, such partnerships are justified by the assumption that public funds are no longer available as they presumably were in the hey-day of urban renewal. More importantly, it is argued that such partner-ships allow for a merger of the best of the public and private worlds as the resources and risk-bearing capacity of the public sector are merged with the innovation and entrepreneurship of the private sector. At a time when laissez-faire economics is more widely celebrated than had been the case in recent decades, public-private partnerships are viewed as the vehicle by which the benefits of private enterprise can be brought to bear on the process of urban revitalization, all of which accounts for the widespread acclaim received by the partnership idea.

A closer look reveals, however, that these partnerships reflect emerging efforts to undermine the public sector, particularly the social safety net it has provided, and to reaffirm the "privileged position of business" (Lindblom 1977) in the face of declining profitability brought on by globalization of the U.S. economy and its declining position in that changing marketplace. Government has a role, but again it is a subordinate one. As Bluestone and Harrison recently argued:

> Leaders may call these deals "public-private partnerships" and attempt to fold them under the ideological umbrella of laissez-faire. But they must be seen for what they really are: the re-allocation of public resources to fit a new agenda. That agenda is no longer redis-tribution, or even economic growth as conventionally defined. Rather, that agenda entails nothing less than the restructuring of the relations of production and the balance of power in the American economy. In pursuit of these dubious goals, the public sector contin-ues to play a crucial role. (Bluestone and Harrison 1988, 107–8)

The continuity reflected by public-private partnerships, despite some new formulations in recent years, is revealed by the persistence in the corporate sector's efforts to utilize government to protect private wealth, and primarily on its terms. Demands on government to subsi-dize a painful restructuring process have placed added strains on pub-lic-private relations. The glue that holds these efforts together, despite these tensions, is the commitment to privatism.

Focusing on the postwar years, this chapter examines the ideology of privatism, its influence on the evolution of public-private partner-ships, and their combined effects on the structural, spatial, and social development of cities in the United States, and the lives of people residing in the nation's urban neighborhoods. Perhaps the most strik-ing feature of the evolution of American cities is the uneven nature of urban development. To many, such uneven development simply reflects the "creative destruction " that Schumpeter (1942) asserted was essential for further economic progress in a capitalist economy. To others, however, the unevenness generated by unrestrained market-based private capital accumulation constitutes the core of the nation's urban problems.

Privatism and the Politics of Urban Redevelopment

The American tradition of privatism was firmly established by the time of the Revolution in the 1700s. According to this tradition individual and community happiness are to be achieved through the search for personal wealth. Individual loyalties are to the family first, and the primary obligation of political authorities is to "keep the peace among individual money-makers" (Warner 1987, 4). Always implicit, and frequently explicit, from colonial days to the present has been the primacy of private action and actors.

Consistent with free market, neoclassical economic theory generally, theory and policy in economic development and urban redevelopment circles have focused on private investors and markets as the appropriate dominating forces. Private economic actors are credited with being the most productive, innovative, and effective. Presumably neutral and impersonal market signals are deemed the most efficient, and therefore, appropriate measures for determining the allocation of economic resources. Given Adam Smith's invisible hand, the greatest good for the greatest numbers is achieved by nurturing the pursuit of private wealth.

Public policy, from this perspective, should serve private interests. Government has an important role, but one which should focus on the facilitation of private capital accumulation via the free market. (Privatism should not be confused with privatization. The former refers to a broader ideological view of the world generally and relationships between the public and private sectors in particular. The latter constitutes a specific policy of transferring ownership of particular industries or services from government agencies to private entrepreneurs.) While urban policy must acknowledge the well-known problems of big cities, it can do so best by encouraging private economic growth. A critical assumption is that the city constitutes a unitary interest and all citizens benefit from policies that enhance aggregate private economic growth (Peterson 1981). Explicit distributive or allocational choices are to be avoided whenever possible, with the market determining where resources are to be directed. Public policy should augment, but not supplant, market forces (Barnekov et al. 1989; Levine 1989).

The ideology of privatism has been tested in recent years by regional shifts in investment and globalization of the economy in general that have devastated entire communities (Bluestone and Harrison 1982; Eisinger 1988). Advocates of privatism attribute such developments primarily to technological innovation and growing international competition. They claim the appropriate response is to accommodate changes in the national and international economy. Given that redevelopment is presumed to be principally a technical rather than political process, cities must work more closely with private industry to facilitate such restructuring in order to more effectively establish their comparative advantages and market themselves in an increasingly competitive economic climate. Such partnerships, it is assumed, will bring society's best and brightest resources (which reside in the private sector) to bear on its most severe public problems.

Where such efforts cannot succeed, cities must adjust, which in some cases means to downsize, just like their counterparts in the private sector. "Pro-people rather than pro-place" policies are offered to help individuals accommodate such changes. These adjustments may well mean moving from one city and region to another. Policies that might intervene in private investment decisionmaking or challenge market forces for the betterment of existing communities are explicitly rejected (President's Commission for a National Agenda for the Eighties 1980; McKenzie 1979; Kasarda 1988).

Concretely, the policies of privatism consist of financial incentives to private economic actors that are intended to reduce factor costs of production, encourage private capital accumulation, thus stimulating investment, and ultimately serve both private and public interests. The search for new manufacturing sites, retooling of obsolete facilities, and restructuring from manufacturing to services have all benefited from such subsidization. During the postwar years cities have been dramatically affected by the focus on downtown development which has generally taken the form of office towers, luxury hotels, convention centers, recreational facilities, and other paeans to postindustrial society (Teaford 1990). Real estate investment itself is frequently viewed as part of the antidote to deindustrialization. All of this is justified, however, by the assumption that a revitalized economy generally and a reinvigorated downtown in particular will lead to regeneration throughout the city. As more jobs are created and space is more intensively utilized, more money is earned and spent by local residents, new property and income tax dollars bolster local treasuries, and new wealth trickles down throughout the metropolitan area. Among the specific policy tools are tax abatements, low-interest loans, land cost writedowns, tax increment finance districts (TIFs), enterprise zones, urban development action grants (UDAGs), industrial revenue bonds (IRBs), redevelopment authorities, eminent domain, and other public-private activities through which private investment is publicly subsidized. The object of such incentives, again, is the enhancement of aggregate private economic growth by which it is assumed the public needs of the city can be most effectively and efficiently met.

Privatism has been a powerful ideological force in all areas of American life. That it has dominated urban policy should come as no surprise. But the pursuit of the private city has had its costs. And the advocates of privatism have had their critics.

Responses to Privatism

The most fundamental challenges to privatism are directed to its central assumptions regarding the neutrality and impersonality of the market. Rather than viewing the market as a mechanism through which random decisions made by many individual willing buyers and sellers yield the most efficient production and distribution of resources for cities and society generally, it is argued that the market is an arena of social conflict. Logan and Molotch (1987) observe that markets themselves are cultural artifacts bound up with human interests. Markets are structured by, and reflect differences in, wealth and power. They reinforce prevailing unequal social relations and dominant values, including a commitment to privatism. Markets are not simply neutral arbiters maximizing efficiency in production and distribution. They are social institutions firmly imbedded in the broader culture of American society.

A related critique of privatism is the argument that a city does not constitute a unitary interest which can best be advanced through aggregate private economic growth, but rather a series of unequal and conflicting interests, some of which are advanced through a political process. As Stone (1987) has argued, local economic development policy represents the conscious decisions made by individuals with highly unequal power in a community in efforts by competing groups to further their own interests. Assumptions of a unitary interest or the benevolence of market-based allocation mystifies important decisions made at the local level which clearly favor some interests at the expense of others. Development, therefore, is not a technical problem but rather a political process. As Stone concludes, "urban politics still matters" (1987, 4).

While economic development and urban redevelopment are political matters, one consequence of the pursuit of the private city has been a reduction in the public debate over development policy and the accountability of public officials and other actors for the consequences of their activities. Quasi-public redevelopment authorities have provided selected private investors with responsibilities traditionally vested in the public sector. Hidden incentives have been provided through such off-budget subsidies as industrial revenue bonds and bailouts for large but failing firms. Eminent domain rights have been granted to and exercised for private interests where public interests are most vaguely identified (Barnekov et al. 1989). The beneficiaries of these policies include real estate developers, commercial business interests, manufacturers and others who view the city primarily in terms of the exchange value of its land at the expense of the majority for whom the city offers important use values as a place to live, work, and play (Logan and Molotch 1987). But it is not just the immediate beneficiaries who share this view of local governance. As Gottdiener concluded, "The reduction of the urban vision to instrumental capital growth, it seems, gains hegemony everywhere" (Gottdiener 1986, 287).

Declining accountability may be a factor contributing to a more concrete challenge to privatism. Simply put, it has not worked. That is the array of subsidies and related supply-side incentives have not created the anticipated number of jobs or jobs for the intended recipients, tax revenues have not been stabilized as initially expected, and the urban renaissance remains, at best, a hope for the future (Center for Community Change 1989; Levine 1987; Barnekov et al. 1989). While not always ineffective, such incentives are not primary determinants of private investment decisions. And they often embody unintended costs resulting in minus-sum situations as public subsidies outrun subsequent public benefits (Eisinger 1988, 200–24). One reason for the disappointing results is that with the proliferation of incentives, the competitive advantage provided by any particular set of subsidies is quickly lost when other communities match them. The number of state location incentive programs alone increased from 840 in 1966 to 1633 in 1985 (Eisinger 1988, 19). Indeed many states and municipalities feel obligated to offer additional incentives of acknowledged questionable value simply to keep up with their neighbors and provide symbolic assurance that they offer a good business climate. As Detroit Mayor Coleman Young observed: "Those are the rules and I'm going by the goddamn rules. This suicidal outthrust competition among the states has got to stop but until it does, I mean to compete. It's too bad we have a system where dog eats dog and the devil takes the hindmost. But I'm tired of taking the hindmost" (Greider 1978). Ironically, one of the costs is the reduced ability of local municipalities to provide the public services that are far more critical in assuring a favorable climate for the operation of successful businesses. For example, in Detroit, perhaps the most deindustrialized and devastated big city in the nation, the quality of public education has declined precipitously in recent years, undercutting the ability of that city's youth to compete for jobs and the city's ability to attract employers (Thomas 1989).

Another factor contributing to the disappointing results strikes at the heart of the ideology of privatism. As Bluestone and Harrison concluded in discussing such approaches to reindustrialization, "all share a studied unwillingness to question the extent to which conventional private ownership of industry and the more-or-less unbridled pursuit of private profit might be the causes of the problem" (1982, 230).

If privatism has not generated the anticipated positive outcomes, it has generated a host of social costs that are either ignored or accepted by its proponents as an inevitable price to be paid for progress. Job loss and declining family income resulting from a plant closing are just the most obvious direct costs. But there are "multiplier effects." Economic stress within the family often leads to family conflicts, including physical abuse frequently culminating in divorce. Increasing physical and medical health problems, including growing suicide rates, have been clearly connected to sudden job loss. The economic stability of entire communities and essential public services have been crippled (Bluestone and Harrison 1982). Even the winners of the competition have suffered severe social costs. Sudden growth has generated unmanageable traffic congestion and skyrocketing housing costs often forcing families out of their homes and business to pay higher salaries for competent employees (Dreier et al. 1988). Gentrification moves many poor people around but does little to reduce poverty. Even in Houston, the "free enterprise city," sudden private economic growth has generated serious problems in sewage and garbage disposal, flooding, air and water pollution, congestion, and related problems (Feagin 1988). Perhaps the most destructive aspect of this "creative" process is the uneven nature of the spatial development of cities and the growing inequality associated with race and class (Bluestone and Harrison 1988; Galster and Hill 1992; Goldsmith and Blakely 1992). These costs are real, but not inevitable. According to the critics of privatism, they reflect political conflicts, not natural outcomes of ultimately beneficial market forces.

The pursuit of the private city appears to have produced many ironies. Given the array of incentives, those firms intending to expand or relocate anyway often shop around for the best deal they can get. Consequently, local programs designed to leverage private investment are turned on their head. That is the private firms leverage public funds for their own development purposes; and they can punish local governments that are not forthcoming with generous subsidies. A logical consequence of these developments is that private economic growth has become its own justification. As William E. Connolly observed:

[A]t every turn barriers to growth become occasions to tighten social control, to build new hedges around citizen rights, to insulate bureaucracies from popular pressures while opening them to corporate influence, to rationalize work processes, to impose austerity on vulnerable constituencies, to delay programs for environmental safety, to legitimize military adventures abroad. Growth, previously seen as the means to realization of the good life, has become a system imperative to which elements of the good life are sacrificed. (1983, 23–24)

But perhaps these outcomes are not ironic. In fact, they may well be the intended results. As Barnekov and his colleagues concluded in evaluating privatism in the 1980s, "The overriding purpose of the 'new privatism' was not the regeneration of cities but rather the adaptation of the urban landscape to the spatial requirements of a post-industrial economy" (1989, 12). That adaptation, as Bluestone and Harrison (1988) noted, has been the central objective of public-private partnerships in urban America.

The postwar debate over privatism, like debates over redevelopment in general, have taken place within the context of dramatic structural changes in the political economy of American cities. The spatial development of urban America has clearly been influenced by these changes. In turn the structural and spatial developments of cities have given rise to a host of social problems with which policy makers continue to wrestle.

Structural, Spatial, and Social Development

Urban Renewal and the Prosperous Postwar Years

The United States emerged from World War II as a growing and internationally dominant economic power. Given its privileged structural position at that time, the end of ideology was declared and optimism for future growth and prosperity was widespread (Bell 1960).

Yet blighted conditions within the nation's central cities posed problems for residents trapped in poverty and for local businesses threatened by conditions within and immediately surrounding the downtown business center. Recognizing the "higher uses" (i.e., more profitable for developers and related businesses) for which such land could be utilized, a policy of urban renewal evolved which brought together local business and government entities in working partnerships with the support of the federal government. At the same time, as indicated in chapter 3, federal housing policy and highway construction stimulated homeownership and opened up the suburbs, while reinforcing the racial exclusivity of neighborhoods.

Though urban renewal was launched and initially justified as an effort to improve the housing conditions of low-income urban residents, it quickly became a massive public subsidy for private business development, particularly downtown commercial real estate interests (Hays 1985, 173–91; Barnekov et al. 1989, 39–48). Shopping malls, office buildings, and convention centers rather than housing became the focus of urban renewal programs. Following the lead of the Allegheny Conference on Community Development formed in Pittsburgh in 1943, coalitions of local business leaders were organized in most large cities to encourage public subsidization of downtown development. Examples include the Greater Milwaukee Committee, Central Atlanta Progress, Inc., Greater Philadelphia Movement, Cleveland Development Foundation, Detroit Renaissance, the Vault (Boston), the Blyth-Zellerback Committee (San Francisco), the Greater Baltimore Committee, and the Chicago Central Area Committee. Using their powers of eminent domain, city officials generally would assemble land parcels and provide land cost writedowns for private developers. In the process local business associations frequently operated as private governments as they designed and implemented plans which had dramatic public consequences but did so with little public accountability.

If such developments were justified rhetorically as meeting important public needs, indeed urban renewal took sides and not all sides were represented in the planning process (Friedman 1968). Some people were forcefully relocated so that others could benefit. According to one estimate, by 1967 urban renewal had destroyed 404,000 housing units, most of which had been occupied by low-income tenants, while just 41,580 replacement units for low- and moderate-income families were built (Friedland 1983, 85). As Chester Hartman concluded, "the aggregate benefits are private benefits that accrue to a small, select segment of the city's elite 'public,' while the costs fall on those least able to bear them" (Hartman 1974, 183).

At the same time that the public sector was subsidizing downtown commercial development, it was also subsidizing homeownership and highway construction programs to stimulate suburban development as noted in chapter 3. Through Federal Housing Administration (FHA), Veterans Administration (VA), and related federally subsidized and insured mortgage programs launched around the war years, long-term mortgages requiring relatively low downpayments made home ownership possible for many families who previously could not afford to buy. With the federal insurance, lenders were far more willing to make such loans (Jackson 1985; Hays 1985). (An equally if not more compelling factor leading to the creation of these programs was the financial assistance they provided to real estate agents, contractors, financial institutions, and other housing-related industries [Hays

1985].) Since half the FHA and VA loans made during the 1950s and 1960s financed suburban housing, the federal government began, perhaps unwittingly, to subsidize the exodus from central cities to suburban rings that characterized metropolitan development during these decades (Hays 1985, 215). The Interstate Highway Act of 1956 launching construction of the nation's high speed roadway system further subsidized and encouraged that exodus.

A significant feature of these developments was the racial exclusivity that was solidified in part because the federal government encouraged it. With the FHA warning of "inharmonious racial or nationality groups," the federal government assured that properties would "continue to be occupied by the same social and racial classes" (Jackson 1985, 208). If redlining practices originated within the nation's financial institutions, the federal government sanctioned and reinforced such discriminatory practices at a critical time in the history of suburban development. The official stance of the federal government has changed in subsequent decades, but the patterns established by these policies have proven to be difficult to alter.

During the prosperous postwar years of the 1950s and 1960s, urban redevelopment strategies were shaped by public-private partnerships. But the private partner dominated as the public sector's role consisted principally of "preparing the ground for capital." Spatially, the focus was on downtown and the suburbs. Socially, the dominant feature was the creation and reinforcement of racially discriminatory dual housing markets and homogeneous urban and suburban communities. These basic patterns have persisted in subsequent years when the national economy was not so favorable.

Partnerships in an Age of Decline

Global domination by the U.S. economy peaked roughly twenty-five years following the conclusion of World War II. After more than two decades of substantial economic growth subsequent to the war, international competition, particularly from Japan and West Germany but also from several Third World countries, began to challenge the U.S. position as productivity and profitability at home began to decline (Bowles et al. 1983, 1990; Bluestone and Harrison 1988; Reich 1983). As both a cause and effect of the general decline beginning in the late 1960s and early 1970s the U.S. economy experienced significant shifts out of manufacturing and into service industries. Between 1979 and 1987 the U.S. economy lost 1.9 million manufacturing jobs and gained 13.9 million in the service sector (Mishel and Simon 1988, 25). Perhaps even more important than the overall trajectory of decline has been the response to these developments on the part of corporate America and its partners in government. Such economic restructuring and the political response provided the context which has shaped the spatial development of cities and, in turn, the quality of life in urban America.

As indicated in chapter 2, the U.S. share of the world's economic output declined dramatically during the postwar years; from 35 percent to 22 percent between 1960 and 1980 (Reich 1987, 44). As profitability began to decline, U.S. corporations responded with an array of tactics aimed at generating short-term profits at the expense of long-term productivity (Hayes and Abernathy 1980).

Rather than directing investment into manufacturing plants and equipment or research and development to improve the productivity of U.S. industry, corporate America pursued what Robert B. Reich labeled "paper entrepreneurialism" (Reich 1983, 140–72). That is, capital was expended on mergers and acquisitions, speculative real estate ventures, and other investments in which "Some money will change hands, and no new wealth will be created" (Reich 1983, 157). Rather than strategic planning for long-term productivity growth, the pursuit of short-term gain has been the objective.

Reducing labor costs has constituted a second component of an overall strategy aimed at short-term profitability. A number of tactics have been utilized to reduce the wage bill including decentralizing and globalizing production, expanding part-time work at the expense of full-time positions, contracting out work from union to nonunion shops, aggressively fighting union organizing campaigns, implementing two-tiered wage scales, and outright demands for wage concessions. Rather than viewing human capital as a resource in which to invest to secure productivity in the long run, labor has increasingly been viewed as a cost of production to be minimized in the interests of short-term profitability (Bluestone and Harrison 1988; Reich 1991; Marshall and Tucker 1992).

If production has been conceded by corporate America, control has not. Administration and a range of professional services have been consolidated and grown considerably in recent years. If steel, automobile, and electronics production has shifted overseas, legal, accounting, along with other financial and related services have expanded at home, particularly in the downtown central business districts of major cities. Other service industries that have also grown include health care, state and local government, and personal services. Such developments lead some observers to dismiss the significance of a decline in manufacturing and celebrate the emergence of a postindustrial society (Bell 1973; Becker 1983). Yet at least half of those jobs in service industries are dependent on manufacturing production, though not necessarily production within the United States. Service and manufacturing are clearly linked; one cannot supplant the other. The health of both manufacturing and services depends on their mutual development. A service economy, without a manufacturing base to service, is proving to be a prescription for overall economic decline within those communities losing their industrial base (Cohen and Zysman 1987).

True to the spirit of privatism, government has nurtured these developments through various forms of assistance to the private sector. Federal tax laws encourage investment in new facilities, particularly overseas, rather than reinvestment in older but still usable equipment, thus exacerbating the velocity of capital mobility (Bluestone and Harrison 1982). State and local governments have offered their own inducements to encourage the pirating of employers in all industries ranging from heavy manufacturing to religious organizations (Goodman 1979; Eisinger 1988). Further inducements have been offered to the private sector through reductions in various regulatory functions of government. Civil rights, labor law, occupational health and safety rules, and environmental protection were enforced less aggressively in the 1980s than had been the case in the immediately preceding decades (Chambers 1987; Taylor 1989). If the expansion of such financial incentives and reductions in regulatory activity were initially justified in terms of the public benefits that would accrue from a revitalized private sector, in recent years unbridled competition and minimal government have become their own justification and not simply means to some other end (Smith and Judd 1984; Connolly 1983; Bender 1983).

The impact of these structural developments is clearly visible on the spatial development of American cities. Accommodating these national and international trends, local partnerships have nurtured downtown development to service the growing service economy. If steel is no longer produced in Pittsburgh, the Golden Triangle has risen, as the city's major employers now include financial, educational, and health care institutions (Sbragia 1989). If auto workers have lost jobs by the thousands in Detroit, the Renaissance Center, a major medical center, and the Joe Louis Sports Arena have been built downtown (Darden et al. 1987). Most major breweries have left Milwaukee, but the Grand Avenue Shopping Mall, several office buildings for legal, financial, and insurance companies, a new Performing Arts Center, and the Bradley Center housing the Milwaukee Bucks professional basketball team, are growing up in the central business district (Norman 1989). With the U.S. economy deindustrializing and corporations consolidating administrative functions, downtown development to accommodate these changes is booming. These initiatives are more ambitious than urban renewal efforts which focused on rescuing downtown real estate. But many of the actors are the same and the fundamental relationships between the public and private entities prevail.

In city after city such developments are initiated by the private side of local partnerships, usually with substantial public economic development assistance in the forms of UDAGs, IRBs, and other subsidies.

As cities increasingly become centers of administration, they experience an influx of relatively high-paid professional workers, the majority of whom are suburban residents (Levine 1989, 26). Despite some pockets of gentrification, most of the increasing demand for housing for such workers has been in the suburbs. Retail and commercial businesses have expanded into the suburbs to service that growing population. To the extent that metropolitan areas have experienced an expansion of local manufacturing firms or attracted new facilities, this development has also disproportionately gone to the suburbs. Extending a trend that goes back before the war years, suburban communities have continued to grow.

The city of Chicago, often labeled the prototypical American industrial city, is also illustrative of the "postindustrial" trends. Between 1979 and 1987 downtown investment exceeded $6 billion as parking lots and skidrow hotels were replaced with office towers, upscale restaurants and shops, and luxury housing (Schmidt 1987). Yet overall during the postwar decades manufacturing employment in the city has been cut in half while it tripled in the suburban ring. Total employment in the city of Chicago in the 1970s dropped by 14 percent, while it increased by almost 45 percent in the suburbs (Squires et al. 1987). It was precisely the continuation of downtown and suburban growth coupled with the decline of urban communities in between which led *Chicago Tribune* columnist Clarence Page to describe his city as having a "dumbbell economy" (Page 1987).

Throughout urban America, the rise of service industry jobs has fueled downtown and suburban development, while the loss of manufacturing jobs has devastated blue-collar urban communities. Such uneven development is not simply the logical or natural outcome of impersonal market forces. These patterns also reflect conscious decisions that have been made, in both the public and private sectors, in accordance with the logic of privatism, to further certain interests at the expense of others. Ideology has remained very much alive. Consequently, serious social costs have been paid.

Many of the social costs of both sudden economic decline and dramatic growth have been fully documented. As indicated above they include a range of economic and social strains for families, mental and physical health difficulties for current and former employees, fiscal crises for cities, and a range of environmental and community development problems. Among the more intangible yet clearly most consequential costs have been a reduction in the income of the average family and increasing inequality among wage earners and their families.

Uneven economic and spatial development of cities have yielded unequal access to income and wealth for city residents.

For approximately thirty years after World War II family income increased and the degree of income inequality remained fairly constant. These trends turned around in the mid 1970s. As indicated earlier, during the 1980s the vast majority of Americans experienced a decline in the buying power of their family incomes. Increasing numbers of Americans are working full time (forty hours per week or more year round) and are earning poverty-level wages. John E. Schwarz and Thomas J. Volgy estimate that nearly 30 million Americans live in families where the bread winner works full time but cannot afford the basic necessities of food, housing, clothing, and medical care. Forty percent of all year-round full-time workers earn less than the poverty level for a family of four (Schwarz and Volgy 1992, 3–15). It bears repeating that families in the lower 80 percent of the income distribution (four out of five families) were able to purchase fewer goods with their incomes by the end of the eighties than they were able to do just ten years earlier. The most severely affected were those in the bottom tenth who experienced a drop of 14.8 percent in the buying power of their income. Only those in the top tenth experienced a significant increase which, for them, was 16.5 percent. (Families in the 9th decile experienced a 1.0 percent increase). Most of this increase went to families in the upper 1 percent who enjoyed a gain of 49.8 percent. While GNP grew during these years and the purchasing power of the average family income increased by 2.2 percent, the top 20 percent received all of the net increase and more, reflecting the increasing inequality. Again, a substantial majority experienced a net decrease in the purchasing power of their family incomes (Levy 1987, 17; Mishel and Simon 1988, 6; Gottdiener 1990).

This growing inequality in the nation's income distribution reflects two basic trends. First is the shift from relatively high-paid manufacturing positions to lower-paid service jobs. While service sector jobs include some highly paid professional positions, the vast majority of service jobs are low-paid, unskilled jobs. To illustrate, the Bureau of Labor Statistics projects an increase of approximately 250,000 computer systems analysts between 1986 and 2000 but more than 2.5 million jobs for waiters, waitresses, chambermaids and doormen, clerks, and custodians. There have also been income declines within industrial sectors reflecting the second trend, noted above, which is the increasingly successful efforts by U.S. corporations to reduce the wage bill (Bluestone and Harrison 1988).

Perhaps more problematic has been the growing racial gap. Racial disparities did decline in the first two decades following the war. Between 1947 and 1971 median black family income rose gradually from 51 percent to 61 percent of the white median. It fluctuated for a few years reaching 61 percent again in 1975 but dropping consistently to 57 percent in 1991 (U.S. Bureau of the Census 1976, 1989, 1992). For black men between the ages of 25 and 64 the gap improved between 1960 and 1980 from 49 percent to 64 percent, but dropped to 62 percent by 1987 (Jaynes and Williams 1989, 28). Within cities, and particularly big cities, the racial gaps have grown larger. As indicated in chapter 2, between 1968 and 1991 black median family income in metropolitan areas dropped from just under 64 percent to just over 57 percent of the white median. And in metropolitan areas with over one million people, the ratio within the central city dropped from just under 70 percent to 57 percent.

Racial disparities in family wealth are even more dramatic. The median wealth of black households is less than 9 percent of the white household median. At each level of income and educational attainment, blacks control far fewer assets than do whites. Among those with monthly incomes below $900 black net worth is 1 percent that of whites with similar incomes. Education helps but does not close the gap. Among college-educated householders 35 years of age or less with incomes over $48,000 annually, black net worth is 93 percent that of whites (Jaynes and Williams 1989, 276, 292).

Not only are blacks and whites separated economically, but racial segregation in the nation's housing markets persists as indicated in chapter 3. Again, during the 1970s the degree of racial isolation in the nation's major cities remained virtually unchanged according to several statistical measures leading two University of Chicago sociologists to identify sixteen cities as "hypersegregated" (Massey and Denton 1993, 74–78). Among the consequences are unequal access to areas where jobs are being created and inequitable distribution of public services including education for minorities, and heightened racial tensions and conflicts for all city residsents (Orfield 1987).

Not surprisingly, it is predominantly black neighborhoods that have been most adversely effected by the uneven development of U.S. cities. For example, in Chicago between 1963 and 1977 the city experienced a 29 percent job loss, but predominantly black communities lost 45 percent of all jobs. Poverty has grown much faster in central cities than in suburban and nonmetropolitan areas with the greatest increases occurring in larger cities with large minority populations. Racial minorities are also more highly concentrated in poor neighborhoods. In 1989 40 percent of poor whites living in cities resided in highly concentrated poverty areas, compared with 71 percent of poor black city residents (Goldsmith and Blakely 1992, 48). The increasing incidence of crime, drug abuse, teenage pregnancy, school dropout rates, and other indicators of so-called underclass behavior, are clearly linked to the deindustrialization, disinvestment, and isolation of city neighborhoods outside the central business district (Harris and Wilkins 1988; Wilson 1987; Goldsmith and Blakely 1992). As Goldsmith and Blakely concluded:

> the restructuring of metropolitan residential areas whitened the already white suburbs and further concentrated African Americans and Latinos in darker-skinned central city areas; wealth and income went to the suburbs and poverty was crowded in the city. African-American and Latino suburbanization has been much slower and more partial than the white dispersal, and it has ended in most cases in resegregation in the suburbs. These geographic changes have had enormous consequences for politics and public finance at all levels in America by isolating not only rich and poor, but dark-skinned people from light. Suburbanization has provided a principal mechanism for sorting out winners and losers, for assigning to different groups extra benefits and costs of restructuring of the economy. Not only do some winners find their way (fairly or not) to higher pay, but once there, they solidify their gains by separation. (1992, 125)

The Continuing Significance of Race and Class

Growing racial disparities in urban America reflect a complex set of behaviors including racial effects of actions initiated for economic and political reasons arguably not racially motivated as well as overt bigotry and acts of intentional racial discrimination. The dynamics of class and race are integral elements in the uneven development of cities across regions of the nation as well as within individual metropolitan areas.

Capital mobility within and among cities has clearly had disproportionately adverse effects on racial minorities. Minorities are concentrated in the inner city neighborhoods, blue-collar occupations, and manufacturing industries that have been hardest hit by deindustrialization, and owning a relatively small share of equity in U.S. business they have received relatively few of the profits generated by such creative destruction (Squires 1984; Goldsmith and Blakely 1992). At the same time, when some corporations seek out locations for new sites, racial composition is one factor that is explicitly taken into account, with predominantly white communities favored, at least in part because of a desire to avoid equal employment opportunity problems (Stuart 1983; Cole and Deskins 1988). Stereotypical assumptions employers hold about blacks, particularly those residing in central cities, also contribute directly to discriminatory employment decisions, as discussed in chapter 2 (Kirschenman and Neckerman 1991; Turner and Fix 1991).

Within metropolitan areas unequal access to business and mortgage loans and property insurance contributes to uneven development, adversly affecting racial minorities. No doubt to some extent these patterns reflect the differential risk that financial institutions confront in various neighborhoods and the fact that minorities, on average, earn lower incomes, own fewer assets, and live in older communities than whites. Yet, as the previous chapter documented, numerous studies have found that even after taking into consideration such nonracial factors as economic status, neighborhood characteristics, and housing conditions, disparities remain in the number of loans and insurance policies in black and white neighborhoods and black applicants are much more likely to be rejected by banks than whites. The story of Reggie Williams is illustrative.

In 1987 Reggie Williams, a black entrepreneur in St. Louis, applied to several banks for a $325,000 loan to purchase land and build a facility for his own oil-change operation in that city. After being rejected by several banks, Williams turned to Bruce Ring, a white developer who had no problem securing a $1.5 million loan on the same land. Ring proceeded to finance Williams and concluded, "No question about it. Reggie should have been able to go through a bank for financing" (Updegrave 1989, 160).

Uneven structural and spatial development of cities adversely affects racial minorities. But racial inequalities in U.S. cities are not simply artifacts of those structural and spatial developments. Racism has its own dynamic. Blacks who have earned all the trappings of middle-class life in terms of a professional occupation, four-bedroom house, and designer clothes, are still routinely subject to demeaning behavior that takes such forms as name calling on the streets by anonymous passers-by, discourteous service in restaurants and stores, and harassment on the part of police, all simply because of their race (Feagin 1991; Anderson 1990). In 1992 Cornel West, director of Afro-American Studies at Princeton University, was late for an appointment to have his photograph taken for his recent book *Race Matters* because ten Manhatten cabs bypassed him and he was forced to take the subway. This was nothing new for West. Several years ago when he was stopped by a policeman on false charges of trafficking in cocaine and he informed the officer that he was a professor of religion. The policeman responded "Yeh, and I'm the Flying Nun. Let's go, nigger!" Within his first ten days of arriving at Princeton he was stopped by police officers three times for driving too slowly on a residential street (West 1993, x). Racially motivated violence in Bensenhurst and Howard Beach, Sambo parties and other racially derogatory behavior on several college campuses, and letter bombings of civil rights lawyers and judges confirm the continuity of vicious racism. The dynamics of class and race remain very difficult to disentangle, but the effects of both are all too real in urban America.

Milwaukee: A Case Study

During the post–World War II years the Milwaukee metropolitan area has exhibited how the ideology of privatism generally and the role of public-private partnerships in particular have shaped the uneven structural, spatial, and social development of cities throughout the United States. A once proud manufacturing center, Milwaukee has experienced a dramatic decline in its manufacturing base and a rise in service employment. As in other cities, redevelopment initiatives focusing on downtown revitalization and, more recently, adaptation to the emerging postindustrial world, have generated pockets of prosperity amidst growing poverty. Today downtown Milwaukee and the suburbs are thriving while many communities throughout the balance of the city are hurting. Inequality, particularly along racial lines, has been exacerbated in recent years. Currently the city is struggling to deal with these issues. The case of Milwaukee concretely illustrates the dynamics of uneven development in urban America during the postwar years.

Milwaukee emerged from World War II as a growing and prosperous city. That prosperity was rooted in the city's durable goods manufacturing industries. By World War II Milwaukee was a world leader in the production of heavy manufacturing equipment. During the war Milwaukee machine shops did most of the metalwork required for the atom bomb project (Norman 1989). While Milwaukee's economy was sound at the conclusion of hostilities, as in many other cities downtown was deteriorating.

In 1948 "a bank president, an attorney, a theatre executive, two retailers, and several industrialists gathered in a downtown bank" to organize the Greater Milwaukee Committee (GMC) primarily for the purpose of revitalizing the central business district (Norman 1989, 183). Formally, this partnership operated primarily through private channels until 1973 when it created the Milwaukee Redevelopment Corporation in order to direct increasing local and federal dollars for urban development into private development projects. In 1986 Milwaukee's commissioner for city development stated, "Partnership. That word seems to apply to nearly every significant accomplishment of the Department of City Development" (Department of City Development 1986, 2). Downtown Milwaukee has indeed been revitalized. But there is far more to the story.

In the mid 1970s Milwaukee began to experience the loss of critical pieces of its manufacturing base. Household names like Allis-

Chalmers, Allen-Bradley, Schlitz, and American Motors shut down, reduced operations, or shifted production to other parts of the nation and the world (Marchetti 1980). Between 1975 and 1985 Milwaukee lost 27,000 manufacturing jobs (Department of City Development 1987) and despite a slowdown in the rate of loss, the decline continued through the late 1980s (White et al. 1989, 9). For the decade of the 1980s the city lost 27,500 manufacturing jobs. While Milwaukee gained 19,000 service jobs, overall the city lost 3 percent of its job base in the 1980s. During these years the suburbs experienced a 20 percent increase (Binkley and White 1991).

In response to the loss of manufacturing jobs, the city focused its redevelopment efforts on the downtown central business district. Milwaukee's "comeback" was kicked off in the early 1980s with the opening of the Grand Avenue Mall, a 250,000 square-foot indoor shopping center that involved the renovation of buildings on three city blocks and construction of skywalks connecting the stores and the mall with surrounding office buildings. The partnership making the Grand Avenue possible involved a $12.6 million UDAG, a $20 million contribution by the city raised through municipal bonds and the creation of a tax-increment finance district, over $15 million invested by the Rouse Corporation, and $20 million provided by 47 local corporations (Norman 1989, 192–95). The mall was followed by many more downtown developments including the Bradley Center noted above, the Milwaukee Center developed by Trammel Crow featuring a luxury hotel and several restaurants and theatres, a Hyatt Regency Hotel, several new corporate office buildings, and many other small commercial establishments. More is on the way. Northwestern Mutual Life Insurance is developing one major office tower while two more will be built by a Washington D.C. developer. Plans are also being considered for expanding the Grand Avenue Mall (Marchione 1990). A key justification for downtown development in Milwaukee continues to be the assumption that revival of the central business district will spill over into the inner city and other residential neighborhoods.

Downtown is booming, and so are the suburbs. Between 1972 and 1987 when total employment in the city of Milwaukee declined by 3 percent from 352,180 to 340,390, employment increased by 33 percent in the suburbs from 396,720 to 531,510 (Southeastern Wisconsin Regional Planning Commission 1989). Even manufacturing employment increased in the suburbs between 1983 and 1987 by 12 percent (White et al. 1989, 10). What has not changed is the racial isolation of the Milwaukee metropolitan area. In 1970 98.5 percent of the area's black population lived in the city of Milwaukee. According to preliminary census counts, by 1990 96.6 percent remained within the city limits. While this meant a slight increase in the black suburban population, it meant little in terms of integration. Much of the black suburban growth was accounted for by the growth of a small black community on the city's north side into one suburb bordering the city on the north (McNeely and Kinlow 1987, 40).

Several social costs have been associated with the uneven development of Milwaukee. Following the national trend, average incomes have been declining. Between 1977 and 1984 the buying power of median household income in the city declined by 12 percent. This reflects, in part, the restructuring of the local economy. The 27,000 manufacturing jobs lost by the city between the mid 1970s and mid 1980s paid an average wage of $23,600, while the 24,000 service jobs it gained during these years paid an average wage of $13,000 (Department of City Development 1987, 14). Compounding these problems is the fact that there are at least seven times as many job seekers as there are available jobs (Wilberg and Wojno 1992).

There are other costs. One critical consequence of the declining economic capacity of many Milwaukee families is the growing unaffordability of housing. Between 1977 and 1984 the median percent of household income spent on rent increased from 26 to 32 percent, while the proportion of renters spending over half their income on rent rose from 15 to 32 percent (Department of City Development 1987, 14, 15). As in many other cities, homelessness has subsequently become a problem in Milwaukee with estimates of Milwaukee's homeless population ranging from 11,000 to 20,000 (Bates 1989, 16). In 1989 Milwaukee experienced a record high of 116 homicides. This was thirty more than in the previous year and twenty-two more than the previous record set in 1987. Local authorities attribute the rising violence primarily to increasing drug related activity in the city (*Milwaukee Journal* 1990, 1).

The spatial segregation of racial minorities in Milwaukee (one of the sixteen cities Massey and Denton labeled hypersegregated) reflects and reinforces other barriers confronting the city's minority population. In its testing programs the Metropolitan Milwaukee Fair Housing Council routinely finds racial steering on the part of local realtors, according to its Executive Director (Tisdale 1992). In the mid 1980s Milwaukee had the highest black to white mortgage rejection rate among the nation's fifty largest cities (Dedman 1989) and the city continues to be among the "leaders" in the early 1990s as black applicants are rejected more than four times as often as whites according to Home Mortgage Disclosure Act reports. Racial composition of neighborhoods still influences accessibility to homeowners insurance and other financial services (Squires and Velez 1987). And during the 1980s black unemployment nearly doubled, while other groups experienced only a slight increase. Black unemployment persists at approximately 20 percent compared to 3 or 4 percent for whites (McNeely and Kinlow 1987, 27).

Milwaukee has experienced many of the social costs of uneven economic and spatial development, including greater inequality. As in other cities, the growing racial inequality reflects both the effects of structural changes and intentional racial discrimination. As an illustration of the latter, the sales manager of a major insurance company recently advised an agent, "Very honestly, I think you write too many blacks. . . . You gotta sell good, solid premium paying white people . . . they own their own homes, the white works . . . black people will buy anything that looks good right now, but when it comes to pay for it next time, you're not going to get your money out of them." The sales manager then went on to refer to a particular customer in the following terms, "he doesn't consider himself as a so-called nigger, just a high class black man" and concluded by advising the agent, "if a guy really wants it, tell him I need an annual premium" (*Ziehlsdorf v. American Family 1988*). The social costs of race and class continue to plague Milwaukee.

Privatism and the policies that flow logically from that ideology have benefited those shaping redevelopment policy, including members of most public-private partnerships. But these policies have not stimulated redevelopment of cities generally. Structural, spatial, and social imbalances remain and are reinforced by the dynamics of privatism. To successfully address the well-known social problems of urban America, policies must be responsive to the structural and spatial forces impinging on cities. At least fragmented challenges to privatism have emerged in local redevelopment struggles in recent years. Alternative conceptions of development, the nature of city life, and human relations in general have been articulated and have had some impact on redevelopment efforts.

Alternatives to the Pursuit of the Private City

In several cities community groups have organized, and in some cases captured the mayor's office, in efforts to pursue more balanced redevelopment policies (Clavel 1986; Clavel and Kleniewski 1990). Explicitly viewing the city in terms of its use value rather than as a profit center for the local growth machine, initiatives have been launched to democratize the redevelopment process and to assure more equitable outcomes of redevelopment policy. Among the specific ingrediants of this somewhat inchoate challenge to privatism are programs to retain and attract diverse industries including manufacturing, targeting of initiatives to those neighborhoods and population groups most in need, human capital development, and other public investments in the infrastructure of cities. A critical dimension of many of these programs is a conscious effort to bring neighborhood groups and residents long victimized by uneven development into the planning and implementation process as integral parts of urban partnerships.

When Harold Washington was elected mayor of Chicago in 1983, he launched a redevelopment plan that incorporated several of these components. The planning actually began during the campaign when people from various racial groups, economic classes, and geographic areas were brought together to identify goals and policies to achieve them under a Washington administration. Shortly after the election Washington released *Chicago Works Together: Chicago Development Plan 1984*, which reflected that involvement. Explicitly advocating a strategic approach to pursuing development with equity, the plan articulated five major goals: increased job opportunities for Chicagoans; balanced growth; neighborhood development via partnerships and coordinated investment; enhanced public participation in decision-making; and pursuit of a regional, state, and national legislative agenda (*Chicago Works Together* 1984, 1). As development initiatives proceeded under Washington strategic plans were implemented that involved industrial and geographic sector-specific approaches to retain manufacturing and regenerate older neighborhoods, affirmative action plans to bring more minorities and women into city government as employees and as city contractors, provision of business incentives that were conditioned on locational choices and other public needs; and a planning process that involved community groups, public officials, and private industry.

Specific tactics included funding the Midwest Center for Labor Research to create an early warning system for the purposes of identifying potential plant closings and where feasible, interventions that would forestall the closing. Linked development programs were negotiated with specific developers to spread the benefits of downtown development. Planned manufacturing district legislation was enacted to control conversion of industrial zones to commercial and residential purposes, thus retaining some manufacturing jobs that would otherwise be lost. As the widely publicized "Council Wars" attested, Washington encountered strong resistance to many of his proposals (Bennett 1988). Conflicts among Washington supporters also occurred when he attempted to transform his electoral coalition into a governing coalition. Despite the many accomplishments, the Washington administration was not able to fulfill its agenda during the less than two terms that he served. The efforts of his administration demonstrated, however, that uneven urban development was not simply the outcome of natural or neutral market forces. Politics, including the decisions of public officials, mattered and those decisions under Washington were responsive to both public need and market signals (Mier 1993; Mier et al. 1986; Giloth and Betancur 1988; Mier 1989; Clavel and Wiewel 1991; Nyden and Wiewel 1991).

In 1983 Boston also held a significant mayoral election. At the height of the Massachusetts miracle the city's economy was prospering and Raymond L. Flynn was elected with a mandate to "share the prosperity." Several policies have been implemented in order to do so.

Boston's strong real estate market in the early 1980s led to a shortage of low- and middle-income housing. Flynn played a central role in the implementation of a linkage program that took effect one month before he was elected. Under the linkage program a fee was levied on downtown development projects to assist construction of housing for the city's low- and middle-income residents. Shortly after taking office, the Flynn administration negotiated inclusionary zoning agreements with individual housing developers to provide below-market rate units in their housing developments or to pay an "in lieu of" fee into the linkage fund. To further alleviate the housing shortage, in 1983 the Boston Housing Partnership was formed to assist community development corporations in rehabilitating and managing housing units in their neighborhoods. The partnership's board includes executives from leading banks, utility companies, and insurance firms; city and state housing officials, and directors of local community development corporations.

Boston also established a residents job policy under which developers and employers are required to target city residents, minorities, and women for construction jobs and in the permanent jobs created by these developments. These commitments hold for publicly subsidized developments and, in an agreement reached by the mayor's office, the Greater Boston Real Estate Board, the Buildings Trade Council, and leaders of the city's minority community, for private developments as well.

The Boston Compact represents another creative partnership in that city. Under this program the public schools agreed to make commitments to improve the schools' performance in return for the business community's agreement to give hiring preferences to their graduates. Schools have developed programs to encourage students to stay in school, develop their academic abilities, and learn job readiness skills. Several local employers, including members of the Vault, have agreed to provide jobs paying more than the minimum wage and financial assistance for college tuition to students who succeed in the public schools.

As in Chicago, the Flynn administration in Boston consciously pursued balanced development and efforts to bring previously disenfranchised groups into the development process. The specific focus was on housing and jobs, but the broader objective was to share the benefits of development generally throughout the city (Dreier 1989; Dreier and Keating 1990; Dreier and Ehrlich 1991).

The Community Reinvestment Act (CRA) passed by Congress in 1977 has led to partnerships for urban reinvestment in cities across the nation, as indicated in the previous chapter. The existence and effective utilization of the CRA by some groups has led to "voluntary" reinvestment efforts by others. An illustrative approach was taken in Milwaukee in 1989. In response to the 1989 study finding Milwaukee to have the nation's highest racial disparity in mortgage loan rejection rates, as noted earlier, the city's Democratic mayor and Republican governor created a committee to find ways to increase lending in the city's minority community. The Fair Lending Action Committee (FLAC) included lenders, lending regulators, real estate agents, community organizers, civil rights leaders, a city alderman, and others. An ambitious set of recommendations was unanimously agreed to in its report "Equal Access to Mortgage Lending: The Milwaukee Plan." The key recommendation in the report was that area lenders would direct 13 percent of all residential, commercial real estate, and business loans to racial minorities by 1992. (After much debate the 13 percent figure was agreed to because that was the current minority representation in the population of the four-county Milwaukee metropolitan area.) Several low-interest loan programs were proposed to be financed and administered by lenders, city officials, and neighborhood groups. Fair housing training programs were recommended for all segments of the housing industry including lenders, real estate agents, insurers, and appraisers. The lending community was advised to provide $75,000 to support housing counseling centers that assist first-time homebuyers. The city, county, and state were called upon to consider a linked deposit program to assure that public funds would go to those lenders responsive to the credit needs of the entire community. Specific recommendations were made to increase minority employment in the housing industry. And a permanent FLAC was called for to monitor progress in implementing the report's recommendations. The report concluded:

> There is a racial gap in mortgage lending in the Milwaukee metropolitan area. Implementation of these recommendations will be a major step in eliminating that gap. The Fair Lending Action Committee constitutes a partnership that is committed to the realization of fair lending and the availability of adequate mortgage loans and finance capital for all segments of the Milwaukee community. Building on the relationships that have been established among lenders, public officials, and community groups, neighborhood revitalization through-

out the city and prosperity throughout the entire metropolitan area can and will be achieved. (Fair Lending Action Committee 1979, 14)

At the press conference releasing the report Governor Tommy G. Thompson "eloquently" stated, "Neither I nor the Mayor are the kind of guys who commission reports only to see them collect dust." The lenders indicated their own institutions and the local trade associations would support the report and implement its recommendations. Representatives of community groups, whose own reports have gathered much dust on bureaucrats' bookcases, nodded approvingly in an expression of most cautious optimism.

Release of the report concluded what had been several months of contentious debates. The unanimous support for the report expressed by committee members at the conclusion did not negate the differences of opinion that prevailed or the fact that compromises were made in the interest of a show of unity. FLAC turned out not to be a permanent entity and the 13 percent goal has not been achieved. But it did lead directly to several other collaborative efforts by lenders, expanded homebuyer counseling programs, new loan products, the creation of the Fair Lending Coalition along with the Milwaukee reinvestment agreements described in the previous chapter. The very existence of the wideranging FLAC report offered some additional hope and stimulated concrete action for revitalization in Milwaukee.

Cities cannot go it alone, of course, nor should it be expected that they could. The uneven development of metropolitan areas and the well-known litany of urban ills have long been the result of state and federal policy and corporate investment practice as indicated above. The increasingly global nature of political and economic activity has directly affected local economies, the spatial development of cities, and various trajectories of inequality—most notably those associated with race. In recent years federal policy has amounted to a direct assault on cities. In 1980 federal funds accounted for over 14 percent of city budgets compared to less than 5 percent in 1992. During these years federal funding to cities for public works, economic development, job training, and transportation were cut by more than 70 percent. Community development block grant funding went from $9.8 billion in 1980 to $3 billion in 1990. During the late 1970s the federal government provided 300,000 new subsidized housing units per year compared to fewer than 30,000 by the late 1980s (Dreier 1993).

Even if these developments had not taken place, there is a need for a strong federal presence due to the interdependency between the wealth and health of the nation generally and its cities. If cities have experienced declining populations in recent years, metropolitan areas still account for 75 percent of the nation's population and receive 83

percent of the its income (Persky et al. 1991, 9). Perhaps more importantly, the concentration and diversity of people in metropolitan areas
have proven critical to stimulate creativity and innovation leading to
the development of new products and services, thus nurturing productive economic growth (Persky et al. 1991, 16, 17). If "edge cities"
constitute an emerging urban form (Garreau 1991) such decentralization embodies many inefficiencies in terms of the new infrastructure
and related public services that must be constructed, which is much
more costly than maintenance of existing facilities (Persky et al. 1991,
21, 22). And while an increasing number of wealthy and middle-class
families "secede" from public life into private suburban enclaves
(Reich 1991), city and suburban communities remain intricately intertwined. One recent study demonstrated that declining cities lead to
declining suburbs (Savitch undated) while another showed that metropolitan areas with the widest disparities between the city and suburbs experienced the lowest rates of economic growth and prosperity
(Ledebur and Barnes 1992). Suburbanites may now constitute a larger
share of voters than city residents and professional politicians may be
able to win elections by ignoring urban issues (Schneider 1992; Edsall
and Edsall 1991). But cities are not disposable products. They remain
essential to the welfare of the nation. As Jane Jacobs argued, "Societies
and civilizations in which the cities stagnate don't develop and flourish. They deteriorate" (Jacobs 1985, 232).

A strong national economy, which facilitates urban development,
obviously requires public and private activity by the state and federal
governments and corporate entities beyond the local level. But there is
also a vital role for such actors in local redevelopment directly. It can
no longer be assumed, if indeed it ever could be, that the rising tide of
a growing national economy would foster balanced development
across geographic areas and population groups. As is the case among
local actors, the key to state or federal policy and broader corporate
initiatives is to nurture investment in wealth-producing assets that
generate balanced and more equitable development rather than speculative ventures (e.g., real estate development, mergers, smokestack
chasing) that amount to little more than Reich's notion of paper entrepreneurialism.

There are four particular areas where public policy and private
investment involving nonlocal entities (though often in conjuntion with
local actors) can effectively address urban redevelopment needs: infrastructure, education, civil rights enforcement, and private investment.

Perhaps no clearer symbol of the decline of U.S. cities is the crum-
bling physical infrastructure. Roads, bridges, mass transit, airports,
sewer systems, school buildings, and other facilities are simply wear-
ing out or falling apart. Yet federal investment in these vital economic

resources has failed to meet current needs. While the nation's population has grown, absolute gross investment in infrastructure has remained constant for the past twenty years. The proportion of federal outlays for infrastructure declined from 5.5 percent in 1965 to 2.5 percent in 1990. This compares, for example, with 13 percent of total central government expenditures in Japan (Persky 1991, 23–25). Such neglect reflects growing demands to cut the federal budget, and particularly to stop "throwing money" at the social problems of the cities, primarily on the part of conservative, Republican businessmen. Ironically, it is the private sector that stands to gain the most from these public investments. Modern airports are now widely recognized as essential for trade, economic development, and the general welfare of the regions they serve. Local businesses will not attract customers if the streets are not safe. Even firefighters are hesitant to enter certain buildings out of fear for their own personal security. A water main burst in downtown Chicago during the summer of 1992 virtually closing down the Loop for several days and costing local businesses millions of dollars. These developments are not inevitable, nor are they freak accidents. While the specific location of such breakdowns may not be predictable, the occurrence of these events can be anticipated with certainty given current levels of investment. Estimates of the nation's capital investment needs range from just under $40 billion to just over $140 billion annually. At the same time, the returns on each dollar of public infrastructure investment will produce two to five times more payoff in economic growth than a dollar spent on tax cuts or deficit reduction (Dreier 1993; Aschauer 1990). Clearly there is a need for greater investment in the physical infrastructure of cities, that investment will serve critical public needs, it will pay off for business, and the federal government must take the lead in producing the required public investment.

In addition to the physical capital, the human capital in U.S. cities suffers from underinvestment. With high school dropout rates approaching 50% in some cities, and racial minorities continuing to drop out at much higher rates than whites, educational systems are clearly in a state of disrepair (Urban Institute 1992; Jaynes and Williams 1989). Given the demands of the emerging global economy for highly skilled professionals, education is increasingly important if the United States is to effectively compete (Reich 1991; Thurow 1992; Marshall and Tucker 1992). The spatial and skills mismatch between the relatively lesser educated, disproportionately nonwhite populations in the central cities and the faster job growth (particularly of those positions where the earnings will support a family) in the downtown central business districts and suburbs makes metropolitan-wide quality education a necessary (though not sufficient) precondition to the development of currently distressed communities (Kasarda 1988, 1990; Kain 1992). State governments, of course, have more direct responsibilities for public education than does the federal government. But if formal education begins with Head Start and concludes with postgraduate training, as appears to be increasingly necessary, the federal government will assume a greater role.

But educating people will simply increase levels of frustration if there are not good jobs at the end of the pipeline. Public policy in this area must be broadly defined to address job creation and access to jobs, along with training for job holders (Urban Institute 1992). As former Labor Secretary Ray Marshall and his colleague Marc Tucker recently argued, what is called for is a coordinated approach to address economic policy, labor market policy, and education (Marshall and Tucker 1992). Obviously, this demands a strong federal presence.

The nation's wealth remains predominantly in the private sector, however, and private investment is critical for urban redevelopment. But public policy has long influenced, and will continue to shape, private investment. The question is, toward what ends. Federal and, to a lesser extent, state policy can encourage investment in the production of new wealth and good jobs following the principle of linkage discussed earlier in connection with local development in Chicago, Boston, and elsewhere. In the area of welfare reform it is now widely accepted that recipients of public benefits must demonstrate some personal responsibility (e.g., holding or looking for a job, enrolling in school) in order to qualify for those benefits. The same approach should be taken when public benefits are sought by private investors whether they are automobile manufacturers, real estate developers, or the owners of small retail businesses.

Simply, there should be a quid pro quo. The specifics may be negotiated on a case by case basis. For example, a developer might be required to set aside a certain percentage of housing units for low-income families in return for building permits, zoning variances, subsidies, or other public benefits. A manufacturer may be required to give first consideration to job seekers from depressed communities in return for a low-interest loan or tax abatement. Derek Shearer has called for a new Social Compact among various units of government, business, and community groups in which public benefits would be tied to the formation of a strategic plan agreed to by all parties (Shearer 1989). That is, a coordinated approach would be developed in which specific objectives are established. Goals would be clearly identified for the use of any public support. Shearer calls for such an approach to address housing, transportation, education, welfare reform, job training, and relocation assistance. The same approach could be taken towards any particular issue viewed by the local community as the major priorities including crime prevention, drug abuse, and health care as well as those identified by Shearer. More recently, many observers are calling for entrepreneurial government whereby the public sector would steer rather than try to control economic activity (Osborne and Gaebler 1992). If concepts like "market oriented," "customer driven," and "results oriented" government are attractive, as advocated by proponents of entrepreneurial government, the bottom line issues remain: what is produced, who decides, and who benefits.

A thriving national economy featuring prosperous local communities does not assure, however, that all groups will benefit or that they will do so on an equitable basis. A strong civil rights enforcement effort, particularly by the federal government, will remain essential for years to come. Historically, federal civil rights law enforcement agencies have not utilized all the tools at their disposal and the enforcement effort was particularly weak during the 1980s (Govan and Taylor 1989; Liss and Taylor 1991). More effective law enforcement will be essential if racial minorities are to benefit equitably from a growing economy.

These diverse initiatives are illustrative of experiments being launched in small towns and large cities in all regions of the United States. While they constitute an array of programs addressing a variety of problems, there are important underlying commonalities. They are responsive to the structural and spatial underpinnings of critical urban social problems. They are premised on a commitment to growth with equity—the notion that economic productivity and social justice can be mutually reinforcing. And the objective is to make cities more liveable, not just more profitable. A more progressive city is certainly not inevitable, but these efforts are vivid reminders that the major impediments have as much to do with politics as markets.

Beyond Laissez-Faire?

The trajectory of future redevelopment activity is blurred. The ideology of privatism is being challenged. Experiments with more progressive policies have occurred. But no linear path in the overall direction of public-private partnerships in particular or urban redevelopment in general has emerged. Harold Washington was soon followed by a Daley in Chicago. Boston's economy in the early 1990s does not look as promising as it did in the early 1980s and the demand for more incentives to the business community is getting louder in the wake of the Massachusetts miracle (Dreier 1990). Milwaukee's mayor frequently expresses concern about the local business climate as civil rights groups challenge him to respond to the city's racial problems. Redevelopment remains a highly contentious political matter.

The grip of privatism has waned since the height of the Reagan years. HUD abuses, the savings and loan bailout, insider trading scandals, and other manifestations of the excesses of the pursuit of personal wealth serve as reminders of the importance of public sector and community-based roles beyond subsidization of private capital accumulation. Experiments in strategic planning to achieve balanced growth in Chicago, to share the prosperity in Boston, to expand membership in partnerships in Milwaukee and elsewhere, to bolster the physical and human capital of cities, and to steer private investment towards public as well as private needs demonstrate the capacity to conceive a different image of the city and the ability to implement programs in hopes of realizing that image. If it is true that, as Warner concluded, "the quality which above all else characterizes our urban inheritance is privatism" (1987, 202), then the central challenge today is to overcome the limitations of privatism.

6

Toward a More Livable City

... we need to ask whether it is possible to build
urban people into vital communities in a culture
whose economic institutions are operated for private gain by their owners, with little or no acceptance of responsibility for the quality of social living? To the extent that social science believes that
this is possible, how does it see that we can do it
and what does it propose? ... With such research
and planning, we may yet make real the claims of
freedom and opportunity in America.

Robert S. Lynd (1939, 246, 250)

If the purpose of intellectual work is, as Paul Baran asserted, "to help
overcome the obstacles barring the way to the attainment of a better,
more humane, and more rational social order" (Baran 1961: 17), then
there are no greater intellectual challenges than the stimulation of real
wealth-producing economic growth, creation of decent and livable
communities, and the eradication of exploitation and unjust forms of
inequality. The intersections of structural, spatial, and social development of cities makes these challenges both more complex yet more
resolvable at the same time.

The complexity is due to the fact that in order to address any of
these issues, each of the other two must be taken into consideration.
Any effort to increase economic productivity or to enhance the quality

123

of urban life in any significant way that does not address the question of racial conflict will be undermined by the ongoing racial strife. Improving the quality of life for the majority of urban residents requires a sound economic base and smoother race relations. (The fact that a privileged few can escape into private enclaves is not the answer for most city dwellers.) And while a thriving economy coupled with progressive urban development policies may not be sufficient to ameliorate racial inequalities, these are almost certainly essential prerequisites.

But the interrelated nature of these problems also means that success in efforts to address any one area may well spill over into the other two. A cycle of decline can be met with a positive trajectory of change. Greater economic productivity can generate more jobs for more residents and more revenues to provide essential public services. These additional resources can (but do not necessarily) lead to a reduction of inequality and the associated conflicts. Similarly, a city that provides quality public services on an equitable basis can facilitate the development of the local human capital, reduce racial and other forms of inequality and conflict, which in turn makes individual residents and the community more productive economically and otherwise—and can contribute to a more prosperous national economy. If racial inequalities and tensions can be reduced, fewer dollars will have to be spent litigating civil rights lawsuits, providing transfer payments, or building prisons. This frees up funds for more productive development purposes which, again, can facilitate local redevelopment and national economic productivity growth.

The previous chapters offered directions and specific recommendations in four particular areas (employment, housing, housing and community development finance, and local redevelopment), reflecting in each case the intersecting dimensions of structure, space, and race and the ideology of privatism that has shaped policy historically. It is difficult to anticipate the contours of specific problems that will arise. But the fundamental elements of future policy responses are suggested by recent efforts to overcome the politics of privatism and the social costs that it embodies. The critical lessons pertain to the values and beliefs on which these policies are premised, the arenas or venues in which debates and actions are conducted, and the methods that are utilized in these strategies for social change.

Values

If the dominant values of privatism are reflected by individualism, materialism, and private enterprise, the values that characterize the challenge to privatism are balanced development, equity, and community. These are not mutually exclusive values, of course. Yet individually and together they constitute a different vision from that of privatism.

Balanced development refers to various dimensions of development including industry (e.g., the importance of retaining manufacturing jobs and not assuming that the service jobs of the so-called postindustrial economy will be sufficient); neighborhood (central city as well as downtown and suburban development); and demography (e.g., racial minorities, women). Economic growth is widely recognized as essential, but it should be growth with equity or, as Mayor Flynn argued in Boston, "sharing the prosperity." This incorporates procedural and substantive changes. Procedurally it requires bringing all those affected by development decisions into the decisionmaking process: employees as well as employers, consumers as well as producers, and residents as well as elected officials and public employees. Substantively, it calls for a more equitable distribution of resources as well as responsibilities. Serving as both an orienting framework and desired result is a belief in the importance of a stronger sense of community that knits diverse interests together.

The ideology of privatism suggests that equal opportunity for all individuals to rise as far as their individual talents and efforts will take them is the proper objective of public policy. Any more raises fear of the presumed trade-off between equality and freedom. But sharp inequalities in the distribution of material wealth undercut efforts to realize equal opportunity. As R. H. Tawney argued over fifty years ago, "opportunities to 'rise' are not a substitute for a large measure of practical equality, nor do they make immaterial the existence of sharp disparities of income and social condition. In the absence of a large measure of equality of circumstances, opportunities to rise must necessarily be illusory. The formal equality of rights between wage-earner and property-owner becomes decorous drapery for a practical relationship of mastery and subordination" (Tawney 1964, 106–7, 111). It is precisely the various forms of mastery and subordination that the concept of equal opportunity conceals which makes it such an appealing ideal to those who reject more direct attacks on inequality. In the face of growing structural inequalities, the ideal of equal opportunity— firmly grounded in the individualism that anchors the ideology of privatism—enables the privileged to see justice in injustice and pacifies many of the victims. Equal opportunity, as the critical legal scholar Alan Freeman observed, is a "myth that rationalizes hierarchy, justifies disproportionate access to goods and power, and shames those at the bottom into internalizing inadequacy" (Freeman 1988, 362–63). Balanced development and growth with equity are values which acknowledge the need to go beyond traditional notions of equal opportunity to assure more equal allocations of material resources and power.

Similarly, a strong community is defined as more than a setting that permits individual upward mobility. As Robert Bellah and his associates argue in their acclaimed book, *Habits of the Heart*, people's ability to develop their individual talents and truly enjoy their own accomplishments depends in large part on the existence of a supportive community. They demonstrate how businessmen and community activists, husbands and wives, and others require both public involvement as well as private attachments—communities with shared memories and common beliefs—in order to thrive. Ironically, however, they show how the privatistic emphasis on individual achievement fragments people's lives, undermines the critical sense of community, and ultimately frustrates their individual desires. It is feared, they cogently argue "that if we give up our dream of private success for a more genuinely integrated societal community, we will be abandoning our separation and individuation, collapsing into dependence and tyranny. What we find hard to see is that it is the extreme fragmentation of the modern world that really threatens our individuation; that what is best in our separation and individuation, our sense of dignity and autonomy as persons, requires a new integration if it is to be sustained (Bellah et al. 1985, 286). Consequently, they conclude, "the individual and society are not in a zero-sum situation; that a strong group that respects individual differences will strengthen autonomy as well as solidarity; that it is not in groups but in isolation that people are most apt to be homogenized" (Bellah et al. 1985, 307).

Balanced development, growth with equity, and a strong sense of community are deeply held values underlying the progressive challenge to privatism. Each reflects a desire for a reduction of inequality in several spheres of social life. If a more equal distribution of resources and responsibilities is advocated, nowhere is absolute equality discussed seriously except by conservatives constructing straw men in efforts to fend off this challenge. But "there are limits to how much social inequality we can tolerate," as David Osborne has suggested (Osborne 1988, 12). The persistent violence in many urban communities, which is increasingly captured on videotape by amateur filmmakers, indicates that the tolerable limits of inequality may in fact soon be reached.

Venue

Solutions to these problems are generally discussed in terms of what government should or should not do. If far too much, or too little, has been expected from government, and if other settings deserve more attention, the public sector, at all levels, does have several important roles to play.

In some areas, particularly civil rights law enforcement, a stronger regulatory stance is clearly necessary. In the area of economic development, at the national and local levels, government can be a valuable partner in nurturing entrepreneurship, in supporting research and development activities to stimulate technological innovation, and in selected cases providing financial incentives to business development where public as well as private benefits are secured. Public investment, of course, is critical to support education (from preschool to postgraduate levels), maintain the infrastructure of metropolitan areas, and meet other social service needs.

But government constitutes only one of several key actors and locations for social change. Other settings include labor unions, the media, educational institutions, religious organizations, civil rights and other advocacy groups and a variety of community-based organizations.

One of the most important struggles to improve the quality of life for the majority of American has occurred at work on the factory floor and in corporate offices. Labor unions certainly have not been free from racial prejudice, corruption, and many other problems. But the labor movement has been vital to increasing the wages of working people, securing fringe benefits like vacations and health insurance that are taken for granted by most people today, improving the health and safety of working conditions from the steel mills to the typing (now wordprocessing) pools, and more recently providing some ownership and control of private capital (Brody 1980; Green 1983).

One reason why organized labor has been able to secure these benefits is because organized workers are often more productive than their unorganized counterparts. Where jobs are more secure and relatively better paid, workers exhibit more commitment to the position. This results in lower turnover rates and reduced personnel costs since fewer people must be recruited and trained. When the cost of labor is bid up (through collective bargaining) employers have greater incentive to maximize the return on their investment by providing their work force with state-of-the-art equipment and the skills to use it. And when given the opportunity, as well as the incentive, to use their skills and experience creatively to improve the production and distribution processes, employers and employees can benefit. As indicated in the discussion of employee ownership and labor law reform, productivity and democratization go hand in hand (Rothstein 1993; Freeman and Medoff 1984).

Perhaps the most important struggle for social change in the nation's history is the civil rights movement. Particularly in the early years, that struggle took place largely on the streets of American cities, at lunch counters, on busses, and in other places of public accommodations. In recent years civil rights activities have taken place primarily in courtrooms, legislative bodies, and executive offices. And while the victories that are most widely remembered are major judicial decisions and civil rights statutes, those victories were won—and the fruits of them were enjoyed—in large part outside the confines of government offices (Weisbrot 1990; Branch 1989; Morris 1984).

Often, these struggles have been carried out in multiple arenas. The community reinvestment efforts illustrate the importance of using legal tools, but also the critical value of support from the media, academic institutions, church groups, and most importantly effective community-based organizations. Similar stories could be told about the labor wars, other civil rights campaigns, and other social reform movements. If the problems of the economy, urban development, and racial inequality are diverse and intermingled, so must be the venues of change.

Methods

If more democratic outcomes are an objective, more democratic means should be employed. At a minimum, this calls for incorporating more people who are affected by decisions into the decisionmaking process. Certainly when it comes to economic policy employees as much as employers have a stake in the outcomes. So do consumers, local officials, community organizations, and virtually every resident from chief executive officers to the homeless. Employee ownership and empowerment at work, joint efforts between neighborhood groups and lenders to stimulate reinvestment, and broader community participation in redevelopment policymaking illustrate some approaches to more equitable partnerships and key steps toward the democratization of both the process and outcome of economic development activities.

Open, honest discussions of common interests and negotiations to resolve conflicting interests often lead to economic productivity growth, urban redevelopment, and amelioration of racial tensions. Frequently government steps in through conciliation, legislation, litigation, or other means to find solutions. But all too often these methods prove to be insufficient. The histories of the labor and civil rights movements, again, are instructive. Strikes, sit-ins, economic boycotts, civil disobedience, violence, and confrontations of various kinds have been utilized to achieve progressive social change. And as previously indicated, if the memorable victories are often favorable court rulings or passage of a new law, reasoned argument and debate are not the only tools that were essential to those triumphs.

If the methods vary, so do the skills to employ them. Obviously, few if any skills are distributed equally across the population. Sometimes entrepreneurial skills are required in order to launch a new business, to assist a local community development corporation, or assure the success of a public-private partnership venture. In other situations, organizing skills are essential to bring attention to and generate action on a problem. In still others hard physical labor is a prerequisite. More concretely, accounting and financial expertise, the ability to write press releases and speak effectively before diverse audiences, the capacity to lift heavy objects, and many other often highly unequally distributed skills are essential.

But these differences do not need to be translated into rigid, structural hierarchies of power and privilege. As Robert Lynd maintained, "If democracy is to continue as the active guiding principle of our culture, it will be necessary to extend it markedly as an efficient reality in government, industry, and other areas of living" (Lynd 1939, 215). If the challenge to privatism is to succeed, the democratic spirit should continue to permeate the methods as well as the articulated values and objectives, or democracy itself will become a mirage.

Freedom, Opportunity, and Individuality

At the moment the United States continues to struggle with its role in an increasingly global economy. Glaring disparities persist between predominantly poor (often working poor) city neighborhoods and ostentatious downtown commercial splendor as well as suburban residential development. In many communities gold coasts and slums still coexist just a few blocks apart from each other. Festering racial conflicts continue to ignite into violence and death.

But points of light exist amidst the continuing blight. There is growing recognition that as the postindustrial age matures, no technological quick fix will resolve these dilemmas. And no matter how hard the victims of these preeminently social processes are punished, there is growing recognition that such an approach will not substantially alter the problematic conditions or behaviors. Also increasingly understood is that by recognizing common interests in a healthy community—at the local, national, and even global levels—and pursuing those ends in an open, democratic way, not only will community life be enhanced, but the claim of freedom and opportunity can be made real, and individualism can flourish as never before.

There are choices to be made. Those choices will determine the quality of life in the nation's cities and around the world.

References

Chapter 1. Restructuring, Place, and Race

Anderson, James, Simon Duncan, and Ray Hudson. 1983. *Redundant Spaces in Cities and Regions*. London: Academic Press.

Barnekov, Timothy, Robin Boyle, and Daniel Rich. 1989. *Privatism and Urban Policy in Britain and the United States*. New York: Oxford University Press.

Bartelt, David W. 1993 "Housing the 'Underclass.'" In Michael B. Katz (ed.), *The "Underclass" Debate: Views From History*. Princeton: Princeton University Press.

Bowles, Samuel, David M. Gordon, and Thomas E. Weisskopf. 1983. *Beyond the Wasteland: A Democratic Alternative to Economic Decline*. Garden City, N.Y.: Anchor Press.

Carter, Jimmy. 1992. Quoted in "Rx For Cities: Involvement, Carter Says." *Milwaukee Journal*, 25 November.

Clinton, Bill. Undated. "A New Covenant for America's Cities." Little Rock: National Campaign Headquarters.

Cole, Robert E. and Donald R. Deskins, Jr. 1988. "Racial Factors in Site Location and Employment Patterns of Japanese Auto Firms in America." *California Management Review* 31 (1): 9–22.

DeMott, Benjamin. 1990. *The Imperial Middle: Why Americans Can't Think Straight about Class*. New York: William Morrow & Co.

DuBois, W. E. B. 1965. *The Souls of Black Folk*. New York: Avon Books.

Fainstein, Susan S., Ian Gordon, and Michael Harloe (eds.). 1992. *Divided Cities: New York & London in the Contemporary World.* Cambridge, Mass.: Blackwell.

Friedman, Milton. 1962. *Capitalism & Freedom.* Chicago: University of Chicago Press.

Galster, George and Edward W. Hill. 1992. "Place, Power, and Polarization: Introduction." In George Galster and Edward W. Hill (eds.), *The Metropolis in Black & White: Place, Power, and Polarization.* New Brunswick: Center for Urban Policy Research.

Gilder, George. 1981. *Wealth and Poverty.* New York: Basic Books.

Harris, Fred R. and Roger W. Wilkins (ed). (1988). *Quiet Riots: Race and Poverty in the United States.* New York: Pantheon Books.

Harrison, Bennett and Barry Bluestone. 1988. *The Great U-Turn: Corporate Restructuring and the Polarizing of America.* New York: Basic Books.

Holland, Stuart. 1986. Personal communications with Gregory D. Squires.

Jackson, Kenneth T. 1985. *Crabgrass Frontier: The Suburbanization of the United States.* New York: Oxford University Press.

Jordan, Vernon. 1991. "Diversity and American Competitiveness." *Focus.* 19 (10): 5, 6.

Katz, Michael B. 1989. *The Undeserving Poor: From the War On Poverty to the War on Welfare.* New York: Pantheon Books.

Kirschenman, Joleen and Kathryn M. Neckerman. 1991. "We'd Love to Hire Them, But . . .': The Meaning of Race for Employers." In Christopher Jencks and Paul E. Peterson (eds.), *The Urban Underclass.* Washington, D.C.: The Brookings Institution.

Massey, Douglas S. and Nancy A. Denton. 1993. *American Apartheid: Segregation and the Making of the Underclass.* Cambridge, Mass.: Harvard University Press.

Mead, Lawrence M. 1992. *The New Politics of Poverty.* New York: Basic Books.

Mishel, Lawrence and David M. Frankel. 1990. *The State of Working America.* Washington, D.C.: Economic Policy Institute.

Mishel, Lawrence and Jacqueline Simon. 1988. *The State of Working America.* Washington, D.C.: Economic Policy Institute.

Mollenkopf, John H. and Manuel Castells (eds.). 1991. *Dual City: Restructuring New York.* New York: Russell Sage Foundation.

Murray, Charles. 1984. *Losing Ground: American Social Policy 1950–1980.* New York: Basic Books.

Orfield, Gary and Carole Ashkinaze. 1991. *The Closing Door: Conservative Policy and Black Opportunity.* Chicago: University of Chicago Press.

Peterson, Paul E. (ed.). 1985. *The New Urban Reality.* Washington, D.C.: Brookings Institution.

President's Commission for a National Agenda for the Eighties. 1980. *A National Agenda for the Eighties.* Washington, D.C.: Superintendent of Documents.

Report of the National Advisory Commission on Civil Disorders. 1968. New York: Bantam.

Sassen, Saskia. 1988. *The Mobility of Labor and Capital: A Study in International Investment and Labor Flow.* New York: Cambridge University Press.

————. (1992. *The Global City: New York, London, and Tokyo*. Princeton: Princeton University Press.

Shaiken, Harley. 1984. *Work Transformed: Automation & Labor in the Computer Age*. New York: Holt, Rinehart and Winston.

Sleeper, Jim. 1990. *The Closest of Strangers: Liberalism and the Politics of Race in New York*. New York: W. W. Norton.

Smith, Michael Peter and Joe R. Feagin (eds). 1987. *The Capitalist City*. Oxford: Basil Blackwell.

Sowell, Thomas. 1984. *Civil Rights: Rhetoric or Reality?*. New York: William Morrow and Company.

Steele, Shelby. 1990. *The Content of Our Character*. New York: St. Martin's Press.

Stuart, Reginald. 1983. "Business Said to Have Barred New Plants in Largely Black Communities." *New York Times*, 15 February.

Tobin, Gary A. (ed.). 1987. *Divided Neighborhoods: Changing Patterns of Racial Segregation*. Newbury Park, Calif.: Sage Publications.

U.S. Bureau of the Census. 1969. *Current Population Reports*. Series P–60, no. 66, "Income in 1968 of Families and Persons in the United States," table 11. Washington, D.C.: U.S. Government Printing Office.

————. 1992a. *Statistical Abstract of the United States 1992*. Table 41, Washington, D.C.: U.S. Government Printing Office.

————. 1992b. *Current Population Reports*. Series P-60, no. 180, "Consumer Income: Money Income of Households, Families, and Persons in the United States: 1991," table 13, Washington, D.C.: U.S. Government Printing Office.

Warner, Jr., Sam Bass. 1987. *The Private City: Philadelphia in Three Periods of Its Growth*. Philadelphia: University of Pennsylvania Press.

Wilson, William J. 1987. *The Truly Disadvantaged: The Inner City, the Underclass, and Public Policy*. Chicago: University of Chicago Press.

Chapter 2. The Changing Context of Race Relations in Urban America

Abraham, Katharine G. 1983. "Structural/Frictional vs. Deficient Demand Unemployment: Some New Evidence." *American Economic Review* 73: 708–24.

Arrow, Kenneth. 1972. "Some Mathematical Models of Race Discrimination in the Labor Market." In Anthony Pascal (ed.), *Racial Discrimination in Economic Life*. Lexington, Mass.: D.C. Heath.

Averitt, Robert T. 1968. *The Dual Economy: The Dynamics of American Industry Structure*. New York: Horton.

Baron, Harold M. and Bennett Hymer. 1971. "The Dynamics of the Dual Labor Market." In David M. Gordon (ed.), *Problems in Political Economy: An Urban Perspective*. Lexington, Mass.: D. C. Heath.

Becker, Gary S. 1964. *Human Capital: A Theoretical and Empirical Analysis With Special Reference to Education*. New York: Columbia University Press.

Bergmann, Barbara. 1971. "The Effect on White Incomes of Discrimination in Employment." *Journal of Political Economy* 79: 294–313.

Blasi, Joseph R. 1988. *Employee Ownership: Revolution or Ripoff?*. Cambridge, Mass.: Ballinger.

Bluestone, Barry and Irving Bluestone. 1992. *Negotiating the Future: A Labor Perspective on American Business*. New York: Basic Books.

Bluestone, Barry and Bennett Harrison. 1982. *The Deindustrialization of America: Plant Closings, Community Abandonment, and the Dismantling of Basic Industry*. New York: Basic Books.

———. 1988. *The Great U-Turn: Corporate Restructuring and the Polarizing of America*. New York: Basic Books.

Blumberg, Paul. 1973. *Industrial Democracy: The Sociology of Participation*. New York: Schocken Books.

Boggs, James and Grace Boggs. 1970. *Racism and the Class Struggle*. New York: Monthly Review Press.

Bonacich, Edna. 1972. "A Theory of Ethnic Antagonism: The Split Labor Market." *American Sociological Review* 37: 547–59.

Bowles, Samuel, David M. Gordon, and Thomas E. Weisskopf. 1983. *Beyond the Wasteland: A Democratic Alternative to Economic Decline*. New York: Anchor Press/Doubleday.

———. 1990. *After the Waste Land: A Democratic Economics for the Year 2000*. Armonk, N.Y.: M. E. Sharpe.

Bradley, Keith and Alan Gelb. 1983. *Worker Capitalism: The New Industrial Relations*. Cambridge, Mass.: MIT Press.

Braverman, Harry. 1974. *Labor and Monopoly Capital: The Degradation of Work in the Twentieth Century*. New York: Monthly Review Press.

Business Week. 1980. "The Reindustrialization of America." Special issue, 30 June.

Carnoy, Martin and Henry M. Levin. 1985. *Schooling and Work in the Democratic State*. Stanford: Stanford University Press.

Carter, Stephen L. 1991. *Reflections of an Affirmative Action Baby*. New York: Basic Books.

Chambers, Julius L. 1987. "The Law and Black Americans: Retreat from Civil Rights." In Janet Dewart (ed.), *The State of Black America 1987*. New York: National Urban League.

City of Chicago. 1984. *Chicago Works Together: Chicago Development Plan*. Chicago: Office of the Mayor.

Cohen, Joshua and Joel Rogers. 1983. *On Democracy: Toward a Transformation of American Society*. New York: Penguin.

Conte, Michael and Arnold Tannenbaum. 1980. *Employee Ownership*. Ann Arbor: Survey Research Center, University of Michigan.

Dewart, Janet (ed.). 1988. *The State of Black America 1988*. New York: National Urban League.

Doeringer, Peter B. and Michael Piore. 1970. *Internal Labor Markets and Manpower Analysis*. Lexington, Mass.: D. C. Heath.

Dreier, Peter and Bruce Ehrlich. 1991. "Downtown Development and Urban Reform: The Politics of Boston's Linkage Policy." *Urban Affairs Quarterly*. 26 (3): 354–75.

Edwards, Richard C. 1979. *Contested Terrain: The Transformation of Work in the Twentieth Century*. New York: Basic Books.

Edwards, Richard C., Michael Reich, and David Gordon (eds.). 1975. *Labor Market Segmentation*. Lexington, Mass.: D. C. Heath.

Ellerman, David P. 1985. "ESOPs and Co-ops: Worker Capitalism and Worker Democracy." *Labor Research Review* 6: 55–69.

Ezorsky, Gertrude. 1991. *Racism & Justice: The Case for Affirmative Action*. Ithaca: Cornell University Press.

Farley, Reynolds. 1984. *Blacks and Whites: Narrowing the Gap?* Cambridge, Mass.: Harvard University Press.

Feagin, Joe R. 1991. "The Continuing Significance of Race: Antiblack Discrimination in Public Places." *American Sociological Review* 56 (1): 101–16.

Freeman, Richard B. and James L. Medoff. 1984. *What Do Unions Do?* New York: Basic Books.

Frieden, Karl. 1980. *Workplace Democracy and Productivity*. Washington, D.C.: National Center for Economic Alternatives.

Friedman, Milton. 1962. *Capitalism and Freedom*. Chicago: University of Chicago Press.

Friedman, Samuel R. 1984. "Structure, Process,and the Labor Market." In William Darity, Jr. (ed.), *Labor Economics: Modern Views*. Boston: Kluwer-Nijhoff.

Galster, George C. and Edward W. Hill. 1992. *The Metropolis in Black & White: Place, Power and Polarization*. New Brunswick: Rutgers University Press.

Geschwender, James A. 1977. *Race and Worker Insurgency*. New York: Cambridge University Press.

Gilder, George. 1981. *Wealth and Poverty*. New York: Basic Books.

Glazer, Nathan. 1975. *Affirmative Discrimination: Ethnic Inequality and Public Policy*. New York: Basic Books.

Goldsmith, William W. and Edward J. Blakely. 1992. *Separate Societies: Poverty and Inequality in U.S. Cities*. Philadelphia: Temple University Press.

Goodman, Robert. 1979. *The Last Entrepreneurs: America's Regional Wars for Jobs and Dollars*. New York: Simon and Schuster.

Gordon, David M., Richard C. Edwards, and Michael Reich. 1982. *Segmented Work, Divided Workers: The Historical Transformation of Labor in the United States*. New York: Cambridge University Press.

Hamal, Harvey R., Economist, Bureau of Labor Statistics. 1988. Letter to Gregory D. Squires, 1 February.

Hearings before the Subcommittee on Economic Stabilization of the Committee on Banking, Finance and Urban Affairs, House of Representatives. 1984. *Industrial Policy*. Washington, D.C.: U.S. Government Printing Office.

Hill, Herbert. 1977. *Black Labor and the American Legal System: Race, Work and the Law*. Washington, D.C.: Bureau of National Affairs.

———. 1982. "Race and Labor: The AFL-CIO and the Black Worker: Twenty-Five Years after the Merger." *The Journal of Intergroup Relations* 10: 5–49.

Illinois Advisory Committee to the U.S. Commission on Civil Rights. 1981. *Shutdown: Economic Dislocation and Equal Opportunity*. Washington, D.C.: U.S. Government Printing Office.

Jencks, Christopher. 1992. *Rethinking Social Policy: Race, Poverty, and the Underclass*. Cambridge, Mass.: Harvard University Press.

Jencks, Christopher and Paul E. Peterson (eds.). 1991. *The Urban Underclass*. Washington, D.C.: The Brookings Institution.

Joint Center for Political Studies. 1983. *A Policy Framework for Racial Justice*. Washington, D.C.: Joint Center for Political Studies.

Judd, Dennis R. 1984. *The Politics of American Cities: Private Power and Public Policy*. Boston: Little, Brown.

Kain, John F. 1968. "Housing Segregation, Negro Employment, and Metropolitan Decentralization." *Quarterly Journal of Economics* 82: 175–97.

Kanter, Rosabeth Moss. 1977. *Men and Women of the Corporation*. New York: Basic Books.

Keating, Dennis W. 1986. "Linking Downtown Development with Broader Community Goals: An Analysis of Linkage Policies in Three Cities." *Urban Affairs Quarterly* 52 (2): 133–41.

Kirschenman, Joleen and Kathryn M. Neckerman. 1991. "'We'd Love to Hire Them, But . . .': The Meaning of Race for Employers." In Christopher Jencks and Paul E. Peterson (eds.), *The Urban Underclass*. Washington, D.C.: The Brookings Institution.

Lafer, Gordon. 1992. "Minority Unemployment, Labor Market Segmentation, and the Failure of Job-Training Policy in New York City." *Urban Affairs Quarterly* 28 (2): 206–35.

Landry, Bart. 1987. *The New Black Middle Class*. Berkeley: University of California Press.

Leadership Conference Education Fund. 1992. "Civil Rights Act of 1991 Enacted into Law." *Civil Rights Monitor* 6 (1): 2–7.

Leadership Conference on Civil Rights. 1985. Information package on Executive Order 11246. Washington, D.C.: Leadership Conference on Civil Rights.

Lichter, Daniel T. 1988. "Racial Differences in Underemployment in American Cities." *American Journal of Sociology* 93: 771–92.

Lieberson, Stanley. 1980. *A Piece of the Pie: Black and White Immigrants Since 1880*. Berkeley: University of California Press.

Lindblom, Charles E. 1977. *Politics and Markets: The World's Political-Economic Systems*. New York: Basic Books.

Lynd, Staughton. 1985. "Why We Opposed the Buy-out at Weirton Steel." *Labor Research Review* 6: 41–53.

Marable, Manning. 1991. *Race, Reform, and Rebellion*. Jackson: University Press of Mississippi.

Mariam, Aster H. 1985. Letter to Gregory D. Squires and attachment from personnel department of employee-owned insurance company in Washington, D.C., 31 October.

Marshall, Ray and Marc Tucker. 1992. *Thinking for a Living*. New York: Basic Books.

McNeely, R. L. and M. R. Kinlow. 1987. *Milwaukee Today: A Racial Gap Study*. Milwaukee: The Milwaukee Urban League.

Mead, Lawrence M. 1992. *The New Politics of Poverty*. New York: Basic Books.

Midwest Center for Labor Research (ed.). 1985. *Labor Research Review*, special issue, "Workers as Owners," 6: 1–114.

Mier, Robert, Kari J. Moe, and Irene Sherr. 1986. "Strategic Planning and the

Pursuit of Reform, Economic Development, and Equity." *Journal of the American Planning Association* 52: 299–309.

Moore, Thomas S. 1992. "Racial Differences in Postdisplacement Joblessness." *Social Science Quarterly* 73 (3): 674–89.

Murray, Charles. 1984. *Losing Ground: American Social Policy 1950–1980.* New York: Basic Books.

O'Connor, James. 1973. *The Fiscal Crisis of the State.* New York: St. Martin's Press.

O'Hare, William P., Kelvin M. Pollard, Taynia L. Mann, and Mary M. Kent. 1991. "African Americans in the 1990s." *Population Bulletin* 46 (1): 1–40.

Orlans, Harold and June O'Neill (eds.). 1992. "Affirmative Action Revisited." *The Annals of the American Academy of Political and Social Science* 523: 1–247.

Persons, Georgia A. 1987. "Blacks in State and Local Government: Progress and Constraints." In Janet Dewart (ed.), *The State of Black America 1987.* New York: National Urban League.

President's Commission for a National Agenda for the Eighties. 1980. *A National Agenda for the Eighties.* Washington, D.C.: U.S. Government Printing Office.

Reed, Jr., Adolph. 1988. "The Black Urban Regime: Structural Origins and Constraints." *Comparative Urban and Community Research* 12: 138–89.

Rehberg, Richard and Laurence Hotchkiss. 1972. "Education Decisionmakers: The School Guidance Counselor and Social Mobility." *Sociology of Education* 45: 339–61.

Reich, Michael. 1981. *Racial Inequality: A Political-Economic Analysis.* Princeton: Princeton University Press.

Reich, Robert B. 1983. *The Next American Frontier.* New York: Times Books.

———. 1987. *Tales of a New America.* New York: Times Books.

Report of the National Advisory Commission on Civil Disorders. 1968. New York: Bantam.

Rist, Ray C. 1970. "Student Social Class and Teacher Expectation: The Self-Fulfilling Prophecy in Ghetto Schools." *Harvard Educational Review* 40: 411–50.

Rosen, Corey, Katherine J. Klein, and Karen M. Young. 1986. *Employee Ownership in America: The Equity Solution.* Lexington, Mass.: D. C. Heath.

Rosen, Corey and Michael Quarrey. 1985. "How Well Is Employee Ownership Working?" *Harvard Business Review* 87: 126–32.

Rosen, Corey and Karen M. Young (eds.). 1991. *Understanding Employee Ownership.* Ithaca: ILR Press.

Rothschild-Witt, Joyce. 1985. "Who Will Benefit from ESOPs?" *Labor Research Review* 6: 71–80.

Rothstein, Richard. 1993. "Unions and the New Administration" *Dissent* (Spring): 159–65.

Russell, Raymond. 1985. *Sharing Ownership in the Workplace.* Albany: SUNY Press.

Ryan, William. 1982. *Equality.* New York: Random House.

Schuman, Howard, Charlotte Steeh, and Lawrence Bobo. 1985. *Racial Attitudes in America: Trends and Interpretations.* Cambridge, Mass.: Harvard University Press.

Select Committee on Small Business, United States Senate. 1979. *The Role of the Federal Government and Employee Ownership of Business.* Washington,D.C.: U.S. Government Printing Office.

Shaiken, Harley. 1984. *Work Transformed: Automation and Labor in the Computer Age.* New York: Holt, Rinehart, and Winston.

Slott, Mike. 1985. "The Case Against Worker Ownership." *Labor Research Review* 6: 83–97.

Sowell, Thomas. 1981. *Markets and Minorities.* New York: Basic Books.

———. 1984. *Civil Rights: Rhetoric or Reality?* New York: William Morrow and Company.

Squires, Gregory D., Larry Bennett, Kathleen McCourt, and Philip Nyden. 1987. *Chicago: Race, Class, and the Response to Urban Decline.* Philadelphia: Temple University Press.

Squires, Gregory D., and Thomas A. Lyson. 1991. "Employee Ownership and Equal Opportunity: Ameliorating Race and Gender Wage Inequalities through Democratic Work Organizations." *Humanity and Society* 15 (1): 94–110.

Swinney, Dan. 1985. "Worker Ownership: A Tactic for Labor." *Labor Research Review* 6: 99–112.

Taylor, Bron Raymond. 1991. *Affirmative Action at Work: Law, Politics, and Ethics.* Pittsburgh: University of Pittsburgh Press.

Thomas, R. Roosevelt Jr. 1991. *Beyond Race and Gender: Unleashing the Power of Your Total Workforce by Managing Diversity.* New York: AMACOM (a division of the American Management Association).

Thurow, Lester. 1981. *The Zero Sum Society: Distribution and the Possibilities for Economic Change.* New York: Penguin Books.

Tidwell, Billy J. 1987. "Black Wealth: Facts and Fiction." In Janet Dewart (ed.), *The State of Black America 1987.* New York: National Urban League.

Tolbert, Charles M. II, Patrick M. Horan, and E. M. Beck. 1980. "The Structure of Economic Segmentation: A Dual Approach." *American Journal of Sociology* 85: 1097–1116.

Turner, Margery and Michael Fix. 1991. *Opportunities Denied, Opportunities Diminished.* Washington, D.C.: The Urban Institute.

U.S. Bureau of the Census. 1969. *Current Population Reports.* Series P-60,No. 66, "Income in 1968 of Families and Persons in the United States," Washington, D.C.: U.S. Government Printing Office, Table 11.

———. 1971. *Statistical Abstracts of the United States 1971.* Washington, D.C.: U.S. Government Printing Office.

———. 1981. *1980 Census of Population, Detailed Characteristics: District of Columbia,* table 231. Washington, D.C.: U.S. Government Printing Office.

———. 1987a. *Current Population Reports.* Series P-60, no. 156, "Money Income of Households, Families, and Persons in the United States: 1985," table 10. Washington, D.C.: U.S. Government Printing Office.

———. 1987b. *Current Population Reports.* Series P-60, no. 157, "Money Income and Poverty Status of Families and Persons in the United States: 1986" (Advance Data from the March 1987 Current Population Survey), table 1. Washington, D.C.: U.S. Government Printing Office.

————. 1992a. *Statistical Abstract of the United States 1992*, table 41. Washington, D.C.: U.S. Government Printing Office.

————. 1992b. *Current Population Reports*. Series P-60, no. 180, "Consumer Income: Money Income of Households, Families, and Persons in the United States: 1991," table 13. Washington, D.C.: U.S. Government Printing Office.

————. 1992c. *Current Population Reports*. Series P-60, no. 464, "The Black Population in the United States: March 1991," table 14. Washington, D.C.: U.S. Government Printing Office.

U.S. Commission on Civil Rights. 1981. *Affirmative Action in the 1980s: Dismantling the Process of Discrimination*. Washington, D.C.: U.S. Government Printing Office.

————. 1985. *Comparable Worth: An Analysis and Recommendations*. Washington, D.C.: U.S. Government Printing Office.

U.S. Department of Labor. 1991. *Employment and Earnings* 38 (1), table 63. Washington, D.C.: U.S. Government Printing Office.

Whittaker, Gerald F. 1977. "Capital Accumulation through ESOPs: A Black Perspective." *Business Horizons* 20: 23–30.

Wilburg, Janice and Mark G. Wojno. 1992. "Expected to Work But No Jobs: Job Availability in Milwaukee." Milwaukee: Social Development Commission.

Williams, D. F. 1976. "Workers' Self-Management and Social Property: A Participatory Approach to Black Economic Development." *The Review of Black Political Economy* 6: 438–67.

Williams, Walter. 1982. *The State against Blacks*. New York: McGraw-Hill.

Willie, Charles Vert. 1979. *Class and Caste Controversy*. Bayside, N.Y.: General Hall, Inc.

Wilson, William Julius. 1978. *The Declining Significance of Race: Blacks and Changing American Institutions*. Chicago: University of Chicago Press.

————. 1987. *The Truly Disadvantaged: The Inner City, the Underclass, and Public Policy*. Chicago: University of Chicago Press.

Wright, Erik Olin. 1979. *Class Structure and Income Determination*. New York: Academic Press.

Zwerdling, Daniel. 1978. *Democracy at Work*. Washington, D.C.: Association for Self-Management.

Chapter 3. All the Discomforts of Home

Applebaum, Richard. 1989. "A Progressive Housing Program for America." In Chester Hartman (ed.), *Housing Issues in the 1990s*. New York: Praeger.

Babcock, Frederick. 1932. *The Valuation of Real Estate*. New York: McGraw-Hill.

Ball, Michael, Michael Harloe, and Maartje Martens. 1988. *Housing and Social Change in Europe and the USA*. New York: Routledge.

Banfield, Edward C. 1968. *The Unheavenly City Revisited*. Boston: Little, Brown.

Bluestone, Barry and Bennett Harrison. 1988. *The Great U-Turn: Corporate Restructuring and the Polarizing of America*. New York: Basic Books.

Bradbury, Katherine L., Karl E. Case, and Constance R. Dunham. 1989. "Geographic Patterns of Mortgage Lending in Boston, 1982-1987." *New England Economic Review* (Sept./Oct.): 3–30.

Bradford, Calvin. 1979. "Financing Home Ownership—The Federal Role in Neighborhood Decline." *Urban Affairs Quarterly* 14 (3): 313–35.

———. 1992. *Community Reinvestment Agreement Library.* Des Plaines, Ill.: Community Reinvestment Associates.

Burek, Deborah M. (ed.). 1991. *Encyclopedia of Associations.* Detroit: Gale Research Inc.

Canner, Glenn B. and Dolores S. Smith. 1991. "Home Mortgage Disclosure Act: Expanded Data on Residential Lending." *Federal Reserve Bulletin* (November): 859–81.

———. 1992. "Expanded HMDA Data: One Year Later." *Federal Reserve Bulletin* (November): 859–81.

Castells, Manuel. 1983. *The City and the Grassroots.* Berkeley: University of California Press.

Checkoway, Barry. 1986. "Large Builders, Federal Housing Programs, and Postwar Suburbanization." In Rachel G. Bratt, Chester Hartman, and Ann Meyerson (eds.), *Critical Perspectives on Housing.* Philadelphia: Temple University Press.

Close, Arthur C., Gregory L. Bologna, and Curtis W. McCormick (eds.). 1991. *Washington Representatives.* New York: Columbia Books Inc.

Community Reinvestment Act Fact Sheet. 1993. Washington, D.C.: National Community Reinvestment Coalition.

Dane, Stephen M. 1989. "Federal Enforcement of the Fair Lending, Equal Credit Opportunity, and Community Reinvestment Laws in the 1980s." In Reginald C. Govan and William L. Taylor (eds.), *One Nation, Indivisible: The Civil Rights Challenge for the 1980s.* Washington, D.C.: Citizens' Commission on Civil Rights.

DeMarco, Donald L. and George C. Galster. 1993. "Prointegrative Policy: Theory and Practice." *Journal of Urban Affairs* 15 (2): 141–60.

"Epilogue—The Costs of Housing Discrimination and Segregation: An Interdisciplinary Social Science Statement." 1987. In Gary A. Tobin *Divided Neighborhoods: Changing Patterns of Racial Segregation.* Newbury Park, Calif.: Sage Publications.

Fainstein, Susan S., Norman I. Fainstein, Richard Child Hill, Dennis Judd, and Michael Peter Smith. 1986. *Restructuring the City: The Political Economy of Urban Development.* New York: Longman Inc.

Feagin, Joe R. 1991. "Killing the American Dream: Discrimination in Housing and Neighborhoods." Paper presented at a national symposium, Race and Housing in the United States: An Agenda for the Twenty-First Century, sponsored by the United Church of Christ Commission for Racial Justice, Atlanta, 6 December.

Feagin, Joe R. and Robert Parker. 1990. *Building American Cities: The Urban Real Estate Game.* Englewood Cliffs: Prentice Hall.

Feldman, M. A. and Richard L. Florida. 1990. "Economic Restructuring and the Changing Role of the State in U.S. Housing." In Willem van Vliet and Jan van Weesep (eds.), *Government and Housing: Developments in Seven Countries*. Newbury Park, Calif.: Sage Publications.

Gilderbloom, John I. and Richard P. Applebaum. 1988. *Rethinking Rental Housing*. Philadelphia: Temple University Press.

Glazer, Nathan. 1975. *Affirmative Discrimination: Ethnic Inequality and Public Policy*. New York: Basic Books.

Gottdiener, Mark. 1985. *The Social Production of Urban Space*. Austin: University of Texas Press.

Gottdiener, Mark and Joe R. Feagin. 1988. "The Paradigm Shift in Urban Sociology." *Urban Affairs Quarterly* 24 (2): 163–87.

Greene, Zina G. 1980. *Lender's Guide to Fair Mortgage Policies*. Washington, D.C.: The Potomac Institute.

Gugliotta, Guy. 1993. "Moving Out of Poverty By Moving Out of Town." *Washington Post*, 24 February.

Harvey, David. 1985. *The Urbanization of Capital*. Baltimore: Johns Hopkins University Press.

———. 1973. *Social Justice and the City*. Baltimore: Johns Hopkins University Press.

Hays, R. Allen. 1985. *The Federal Government & Urban Housing: Ideology and Change in Public Policy*. Albany: SUNY Press.

Hoyt, Homer. 1933. *One Hundred Years of Land Values in Chicago*. Chicago: University of Chicago Press.

ICF Incorporated. 1991. "The Secondary Mortgage Market and Community Lending through Lenders' Eyes." Prepared for the Federal Home Loan Mortgage Corporation, Fairfax, Va.: ICF Incorporated.

Insurance Information Institute. 1991. *1991 Property/Casualty Insurance Facts*. New York: Insurance Information Institute.

Jackson, Kenneth T. 1985. *Crabgrass Frontier: The Suburbanization of the United States*. New York: Oxford University Press.

Judd, Dennis R. 1984. *The Politics of American Cities: Private Power and Public Policy*. Boston: Little, Brown.

Kasarda, John. 1988. "Economic Restructuring and America's Urban Dilemma." In Mattei Dogan and John Kasarda (eds.), *The Metropolis Era*, vol 1: *A World of Giant Cities*. Newbury Park, Calif.: Sage Publications.

Kozol, Jonathan. 1991. *Savage Inequalities: Children in America's Schools*. New York: Crown Publishers.

Labaton, Stephen. 1991. "Administration Presents Its Plan For Broad Overhaul of Banking." *New York Times*, 6 February.

Lamarche, Francois. 1976. "Property Development and the Economic Foundations of the Urban Question." In C. G. Pickvance (ed.), *Urban Sociology: Critical Essays*. London: Tavistock Publications.

Leavitt, Jacqueline and Susan Saegert. 1990. *From Abandonment to Hope: Community-Households in Harlem*. New York: Columbia University Press.

Lefebvre, Henri. 1992. *The Production of Space*. Oxford: Basil Blackwell.

Leigh, Wilhelmina A. and James D. McGhee. 1986. "A Minority Perspective on Residential Racial Integration." In John M. Goering (ed.), *Housing Desegregation and Federal Policy*. Chapel Hill: University of North Carolina Press.

Lief, Beth J. and John Goering. 1987. "The Implementation of the Federal Mandate for Fair Housing." In Gary A. Tobin (ed.), *Divided Neighborhoods: Changing Patterns of Racial Segregation*. Newbury Park, Calif.: Sage Publications.

Logan, John R. and Harvey L. Molotch. 1987. *Urban Fortunes: The Political Economy of Place*. Berkeley: University of California Press.

Massey, Douglas S. and Nancy Denton. 1987. "Trends in the Residential Segregation of Blacks, Hispanics, and Asians: 1970-1980." *American Sociological Review* 52 (6): 802–25.

————. 1993. *American Apartheid: Segregation and the Making of the Underclass*. Cambridge, Mass.: Harvard University Press.

Massey, Douglas S. and Mitchell L. Eggers. 1990. "The Ecology of Inequality: Minorities and the Concentration of Poverty, 1970-1980." *American Journal of Sociology* 95 (5): 1153–88.

Meyerson, Ann. 1986. "Deregulation and the Restructuring of the Housing Finance System." In Rachel C. Bratt, Chester Hartman, and Ann Meyerson (eds.), *Critical Perspectives on Housing*. Philadelphia: Temple University Press.

Mills, C. Wright. 1959. *The Sociological Imagination*. New York: Oxford University Press.

Mishel, Lawrence and David M. Frankel. 1991. *The State of Working America*. Washington, D.C.: Economic Policy Institute.

Munnell, Alicia H., Lynn E. Browne, James McEneaney, and Geoffrey M. B. Tootell. 1992. "Mortgage Lending in Boston: Interpreting HMDA Data," Working Paper Series, Federal Reserve Bank of Boston, October.

National Commission on Neighborhoods. 1979. *People Building Neighborhoods: Final Report to the President and the Congress of the United States*. Washington, D.C.: U.S. Government Printing Office.

O'Hare, William P., Kelvin M. Pollard, Taynia L. Mann, and Mary M. Kent. 1991. "African Americans in the 1990s" *Population Bulletin* 46 (1): 1–40.

Page, Clarence. 1987. Personal interview with Gregory D. Squires, 19 March.

Pearce, Diana. 1979. "Gatekeepers and Homeseekers: Institutional Patterns in Racial Steering." *Social Problems* 26: 325–42.

Phillips, Kevin. 1990. *The Politics of Rich and Poor: Wealth and the American Electorate in the Reagan Aftermath*. New York: Random House.

President's Commission on Housing. 1982. *The Report of the President's Commission on Housing*. Washington, D.C.: U.S. Government Printing Office.

Reich, Robert B. 1983. *The Next American Frontier*. New York: Times Books.

————. 1991. *The Work of Nations: Preparing Ourselves for the Twenty-First Century*. New York: Alfred A. Knopf.

Report of the National Advisory Commission on Civil Disorders 1968. New York: The New York Times Company.

Rosenbaum, James E. and Susan J. Popkin. 1991. "Employment and Earnings of Low-Income Blacks Who Move to Middle-Class Suburbs." In Christopher Jencks and Paul E. Peterson (eds.), *The Urban Underclass*. Washington, D.C.: The Brookings Institution.

Rosenbaum, James E., Leonard S. Rubinowitz, and Marilynn J. Kulieke. 1986. "Low-Income Black Children in White Suburban Schools," Research and

Policy Reports. Evanston, Ill.: Center for Urban Affairs and Policy Research, Northwestern University.

Sassen, Saskia. 1988. *The Mobility of Labor and Capital.* Cambridge: Cambridge University Press.

———. 1991. *The Global City: New York, London, Tokyo.* Princeton: Princeton University Press.

Savings Institutions Sourcebook. 1990. New York: United States League of Savings Institutions.

Schwemm, Robert G. 1989. "Federal Fair Housing Enforcement: A Critique of the Reagan Administration's Record and Recommendations for the Future." In Reginald C. Govan and William L. Taylor (eds.), *One Nation, Indivisible: The Civil Rights Challenges for the 1990s.* Washington, D.C.: Citizens' Commission on Civil Rights.

Shlay, Anne B. 1989. "Financing Community: Methods for Assessing Residential Credit Disparities, Market Barriers, and Institutional Reinvestment Performance in the Metropolis." *Journal of Urban Affairs* 11 (3): 201–23.

Smith, Michael Peter and Joe R. Feagin (eds). 1987. *The Capitalist City.* Oxford: Basil Blackwell.

Squires, Gregory D. (ed). 1992. *From Redlining to Reinvestment: Community Responses to Urban Disinvestment.* Philadelphia: Temple University Press.

Squires, Gregory D. and William Velez. 1987. "Insurance Redlining and the Transformation of an Urban Metropolis." *Urban Affairs Quarterly* 23 (1): 63–83.

Stone, Michael E. 1986. "Housing and the Dynamics of U.S. Capitalism." In Rachel G. Bratt, Chester Hartman, and Ann Meyerson (eds.), *Critical Perspectives on Housing.* Philadelphia: Temple University Press.

Tobin, Gary A. (ed). 1987. *Divided Neighborhoods: Changing Patterns of Racial Segregation.* Newbury Park, Calif.: Sage Publications

Turner, Margery Austin, Raymond Y. Struyk, and John Yinger. 1991. *Housing Discrimination Study.* Washington, D.C.: The Urban Institute.

U.S. Bureau of the Census. 1970. *Current Population Reports.* Series P-60, no. 75. "Income in 1969 of Families and Persons in the United States," table 16. Washington, D.C.: U.S. Government Printing Office.

———. 1992. *Current Population Reports.* Series P-60, no. 180, "Money Income of Households, Families, and Persons in the United States: 1991," table 13. Washington, D.C.: U.S. Government Printing Office.

U.S. Commission on Civil Rights. 1974. *Mortgage Money: Who Gets It?.* Washington, D.C.: U.S. Commission on Civil Rights.

U.S. Department of Housing and Urban Development. 1991. *1990 The State of Fair Housing.* Washington, D.C.: U.S. Department of Housing and Urban Development.

U.S. Federal Housing Administration. 1938. *Underwriting Manual.* Washington, D.C.: U.S. Government Printing Office.

Van Vliet, Willem and Jan Van Weesep. 1990. *Government and Housing: Developments in Seven Countries.* Newbury Park, Calif.: Sage Publications.

Vidal, Avis. 1990. "A Community-Based Approach to Affordable Housing." *Commentator* 2 (2): 1–4.

Wilson, William J. 1987. *The Truly Disadvantaged: The Inner City, The Underclass, and Public Policy.* Chicago: University of Chicago Press.

Wirth, Louis. 1947. "Housing as a Field of Sociological Research." *American Sociological Review* 12 (2): 137–43.

Zarembka, Arlene. 1990. *The Urban Housing Crisis: Social, Economic and Legal Issues and Proposals.* New York: Greenwood Press.

Zukin, Sharon. 1991. *Landscapes of Power: From Detroit to Disney World.* Berkeley: University of California Press.

Chapter 4. Redlining and Community Reinvestment

Art, Robert C. 1987. "Social Responsibility in Bank Credit Decisions: The Community Reinvestment Act One Decade Later." *Pacific Law Journal* 18: 1071–1139.

Babcock, Frederick. 1932. *The Valuation of Real Estate.* New York: McGraw-Hill.

Bates, Timothy. 1989. "The Changing Nature of Minority Business: A Comparative Analysis of Asian, Nonminority, and Black-Owned Businesses." *The Review of Black Political Economy* 18 (2): 25–42.

———. 1991. "Commercial Bank Financing of White- and Black-Owned Small Business Start Ups." *Quarterly Review of Business and Economics* 31 (Spring): 64–80.

Banker, John. 1993. "Let Free Market, Not the CRA, Be the Regulator." *The Business Journal,* 16 January.

Bradbury, Katherine L., Karl E. Case, and Constance R. Dunham. 1989. "Geographic Patterns of Mortgage Lending in Boston, 1982–1987." *New England Economic Review* (Sept./Oct.): 3–30.

Bradford, Calvin. 1990a. "Housing Finance and Race: A Time to End the Dual Market." Unpublished manuscript.

———. 1990b. *Partnerships for Reinvestment: An Evaluation of the Chicago Neighborhood Lending Programs.* Chicago: National Training and Information Center.

———. 1992. *Community Reinvestment Agreement Library.* Des Plaines, Ill.: Community Reinvestment Associates.

Bradford, Calvin and Gale Cincotta. 1992. "The Legacy, The Promise, and the Unfinished Agenda." In Gregory D. Squires (ed.), *From Redlining to Reinvestment: Community Responses to Urban Disinvestment.* Philadelphia: Temple University Press.

Braykovich, Mark. 1990. "Cincy Group Wins Major Reinvestment Agreements." *Disclosure* 119 (November–December): 4–5.

Brown, Jonathan. 1991. Statement before the Committee on Banking, Finance and Urban Affairs of the U.S. House of Representatives. Cited in Calvin Bradford and Gale Cincotta, "The Legacy, The Promise and the Unfinished Agenda." In Gregory D. Squires (ed.), *From Redlining to Reinvestment: Community Responses to Urban Disinvestment.* Philadelphia: Temple University Press.

Campen, James T. 1990a. "Payment Due." *Dollars & Sense* 155 (April).

―――. 1990b. "The Political Economy of Linked Deposit Banking Programs." Paper presented at the meetings of the Union for Radical Political Economics/Allied Social Sciences Associations, Washington, D.C., 28 December.

―――. 1993. "Banks, Communities, and Public Policy." Working Paper Series, Department of Economics, University of Massachusetts at Boston.

Canner, Glenn B. and Dolores Smith. 1991. "Home Mortgage Disclosure Act: Expanded Data on Residential Lending." *Federal Reserve Bulletin* (November): 859–81.

―――. 1992. "Expanded HMDA Data: One Year Later." *Federal Reserve Bulletin* (November): 859–81.

Center for Community Change. 1989. *Mortgage Lending Discrimination Testing Project.* Washington, D.C.: Center for Community Change and U.S. Department of Housing and Urban Development.

Chud, Ann and Hal Bonnette. 1993. "Targeting a Lending Discrimination Investigation." Home Mortgage Lending and Discrimination Conference, U.S. Department of Housing and Urban Development and the Office of the Comptroller of the Currency, Washington, D.C., 18–19 May.

Community Reinvestment Act Fact Sheet. 1993. Washington, D.C.: National Community Reinvestment Coalition.

Comptroller of the Currency. 1993. News Release, "OCC To Use New Examinations to Identify Loan Discrimination," Washington, D.C., 5 May.

Dane, Stephen M. 1989. "Federal Enforcement of the Fair Lending, Equal Credit Opportunity, and Community Reinvestment Laws in the 1980s." In Reginald C. Govan and William L. Taylor (eds.), *One Nation, Indivisible: The Civil Rights Challenges of the 1990s.* Washington, D.C.: Citizens Commission on Civil Rights.

―――. 1991. "Federal Enforcement of the Fair Lending, Equal Credit Opportunity, and Community Reinvestment Laws: 1989-1990." In Susan M. Liss and William L. Taylor (eds.), *Lost Opportunities: The Civil Rights Record of the Bush Administration Mid-Term.* Washington, D.C.: Citizens Commission on Civil Rights.

Dane, Stephen M. and Wade J. Henderson. 1990. "Statement of the Leadership Conference on Civil Rights Concerning Mortgage Discrimination." Hearing Before the Subcommittee on Consumer and Regulatory Affairs of the Committee on Banking, Housing and Urban Affairs of the United States Senate. In *Discrimination in Home Mortgage Lending.* Washington, D.C.: U.S. Government Printing Office.

Dedman, Bill. 1988. "The Color of Money." *Atlanta Journal/Constitution*1–16 May.

―――. 1989. "Blacks Turned Down for Home Loans from S&Ls Twice as Often as Whites." *Atlanta Journal/Constitution*, 22 January.

Elverman, Tim. 1990. Personal interview with Sally O'Connor, 14 September.

Everett, David. 1992. "Confrontation, Negotiation, and Collaboration: Detroit's Multi Billion Dollar Agreement." In Gregory D. Squires (ed.), *From Redlining to Reinvestment: Community Responses to Urban Disinvestment.* Philadelphia: Temple University Press.

Fair Lending Action Committee. 1989. "Equal Access to Mortgage Lending: The Milwaukee Plan." Report of the Fair Lending Action Committee to

Mayor John Norquist and Governor Tommy G. Thompson. Milwaukee: City of Milwaukee.

Fannie Mae. 1992. "Fannie Mae's Fourth Annual Housing Conference Presents Leading Research on Housing Discrimination." News release, Federal National Mortgage Association, Washington, D.C., 19 May.

Fishbein, Allen. 1990a. "Mortgage Lending Discrimination and Fair Lending Enforcement." Hearing before the Subcommittee on Consumer and Regulatory Affairs of the Committee on Banking, Housing and Urban Affairs of the United States Senate. *Discrimination in Home Mortgage Lending.* Washington, D.C.: U.S. Government Printing Office.

———. 1990b. "Mortgage Lending Discrimination and Fair Lending Enforcement." Testimony by Allen J. Fishbein, Center for Community Change, prepared for the Subcommittee on Consumer and Regulatory Affairs of the Committee on Banking, Housing and Urban Affairs, United States Senate. Washington, D.C.: Center for Community Change.

Galster, George C. 1991a. "Black Suburbanization: Has it Changed the Relative Location of Races?" *Urban Affairs Quarterly* 26 (4): 621–28.

———. 1991b. "Statistical Proof of Discrimination in Home Mortgage Lending." *The Review of Banking & Financial Services* 7 (20): 187–97.

Glabere, Michael L. 1992. "Milwaukee: A Tale of Three Cities." In Gregory D. Squires (ed.), *From Redlining to Reinvestment: Community Responses to Urban Disinvestment.* Philadelphia: Temple University Press.

Goldstein, Ira J. 1993. "Methods for Identifying Lenders for Investigation under the Fair Housing Act." Home Mortgage Lending and Discrimination Conference, U.S. Department of Housing and Urban Development and Office of the Comptroller of the Currency, Washington, D.C., 18–19 May.

Greene, Zina G. 1980. *Lender's Guide to Fair Mortgage Policies.* Washington, D.C.: The Potomac Institute.

Greenhouse, Steven. 1993. "Nonbanks Community Role Will Be Target of U.S. Study." *New York Times,* 9 June.

Hoyt, Homer. 1933. *One Hundred Years of Land Values in Chicago.* Chicago: University of Chicago Press.

ICF Incorporated. 1991. "The Secondary Mortgage Market and Community Lending Through Lenders' Eyes." Prepared for the Federal Home Loan Mortgage Corporation, Fairfax, Va.: ICF Incorporated.

Jackson, Kenneth T. 1985. *Crabgrass Frontier: The Suburbanization of the United States.* New York: Oxford University Press.

Judd, Dennis R. 1984. *The Politics of American Cities: Private Power and Public Policy.* Boston: Little, Brown.

Knapp, John J. 1987. Testimony before the U.S. Commission on Civil Rights in *Issues in Housing Discrimination,* vol. 2. Washington, D.C.: U.S. Commission on Civil Rights.

Kushner, James A. 1988. "An Unfinished Agenda: The Federal Fair Housing Enforcement Effort." *Yale Law & Policy Review* 6 (2): 348–60.

Kohn, Ernest. 1993. "The New York State Banking Study: Research on Mortgage Discrimination." Home Mortgage Lending and Discrimination Conference, U.S. Department of Housing and Urban Development and the Office of the Comptroller of the Currency, Washington, D.C., 18–19 May.

Labaton, Stephen. 1991. "Administration Presents its Plan For Broad Overhaul of Banking." *New York Times*, 6 February.

Lawton, Rachel. 1993. "Pre-Application Mortgage Lending Testing Program: Lender Testing by a Local Agency." Home Mortgage Lending and Discrimination Conference, U.S. Department of Housing and Urban Development and Office of the Comptroller of the Currency, 18–19 May.

LaWare, John P. 1990. Statement by John P. LaWare, Hearing before the Subcommittee on Consumer and Regulatory Affairs of the Committee on Banking, Housing, and Urban Affairs of the United States Senate. In *Discrimination in Home Mortgage Lending*. Washington, D.C.: U.S. Government Printing Office.

Leeds, Barry. 1993. "Testing for Discrimination During the Pre-Application and Post-Application Phases of Mortgage Lending." Home Mortgage Lending and Discrimination Conference, U.S. Department of Housing and Urban Development and Office of the Comptroller of the Currency, 18–19 May.

Massey, Douglas S. and Nancy A. Denton. 1993. *American Apartheid: Segregation and the Making of the Underclass*. Cambridge, Mass.: Harvard University Press.

Meyerson, Ann. 1986. "Deregulation and the Restructuring of the Housing Finance System." In Rachel C. Bratt, Chester Hartman, and Ann Meyerson (eds.), *Critical Perspectives in Housing*. Philadelphia: Temple University Press.

Metzger, John T. 1990. "The Community Reinvestment Act in the 1990s: Lessons From Pittsburgh." Paper presented to the National Congress for Community Economic Development, Boston, 11 November.

Munnell, Alicia H., Lynn E. Browne, James McEneaney, and Geoffrey M. B. Tootell. 1992. "Mortgage Lending in Boston: Interpreting HMDA Data." Working Paper Series, Federal Reserve Bank of Boston, October.

National Council for Urban Economic Development. Undated. "The Community Reinvestment Act and Economic Development: A Profile of Community Lending in Eight Cities." Washington, D.C.: National Council for Urban Economic Development.

Norman, Jack. 1992. "Deal to Boost Lending Reached." *The Milwaukee Journal*, 12 February.

———. 1993a. "St. Francis, Coalition Sign Deal." *The Milwaukee Journal*, 25 May.

———. 1993b. "Lenders Get Religion." *The Milwaukee Journal*, 29 June.

Peterson, Margaret. 1990. Personal communication with Margaret Peterson, Loan Officer with Republic Capital Mortgage Corporation, 12 November.

Pizzo, Stephen, Mary Fricker, and Paul Muolo. 1989. *Inside Job: The Looting of America's Savings and Loans*. New York: McGraw-Hill.

Pogge, Jean. 1992. "Reinvestment in Chicago Neighborhoods: A Twenty Year Struggle." In Gregory D. Squires (ed.), *From Redlining to Reinvestment: Community Responses to Urban Disinvestment*. Philadelphia: Temple University Press.

Quint, Michael. 1991. "Big Bank Merger to Join Chemical, Manufacturers." *New York Times*, 16 July.

Relman, John P. 1991. "Federal Fair Housing Enforcement under President Bush: An Assessment at Mid-Term and Recommendations for the Future." In Susan M. Liss and William L. Taylor (eds.), *Lost Opportunities: The Civil Rights Record of The Bush Administration Mid-Term*. Washington D.C.: Citizens Commission on Civil Rights.

The Rockefeller Foundation and the Urban Institute. 1991. "Testing for Discrimination in America: Results and Policy Implications." Conference held in Washington, D.C., 26 September.

Rosen, David. 1992. "California: Lessons from Statewide Advocacy, Local Government, and Private Industry Initiatives." In Gregory D. Squires (ed.), *Redlining and Reinvestment: Community Responses to Urban Disinvestment*. Philadelphia: Temple University Press.

Savings Institutions Sourcebook. 1990. New York: United States League of Savings Institutions.

Schafer, Robert and Helen F. Ladd. 1981. *Discrimination in Mortgage Lending*. Cambridge, Mass.: MIT Press.

Schwemm, Robert G. 1987. "Private Enforcement and the Fair Housing Act." *Yale Law & Policy Review* 6 (2): 375–84.

———. 1989. "Federal Fair Housing Enforcement: A Critique of the Reagan Administration's Record and Recommendations for the Future." In Reginald C. Govan and William L. Taylor (eds.), *One Nation, Indivisible: The Civil Rights Challenge for the 1990s*. Washington, D.C.: Citizens Commission on Civil Rights.

———. 1993. "Housing Discrimination and the Appraisal Industry." Home Mortgage Lending and Discrimination Conference, U.S. Department of Housing and Urban Development and Office of the Comptroller of the Currency, 18–19 May.

Seidman, L. William. 1990. Testimony prepared for the Subcommittee on Consumer and Regulatory Affairs of the Committee on Banking, Housing, and Urban Affairs, United States Senate. In *Discrimination in Home Mortgage Lending*. Washington, D.C.: U.S. Government Printing Office.

Shlay, Anne B. 1989. "Financing Community: Methods for Assessing Residential Credit Disparities, Market Barriers, and Institutional Reinvestment Performance in the Metropolis." *Journal of Urban Affairs* 11 (3): 201–23.

Sloane, Glenda. 1983. "Discrimination in Home Mortgage Financing." *A Sheltered Crisis: The State of Fair Housing in the Eighties*. Washington, D.C.: U.S. Commission on Civil Rights.

Sloane, Martin E. (1983). "Federal Housing Policy and Equal Opportunity." *A Sheltered Crisis: The State of Fair Housing in the Eighties*. Washington, D.C.: U.S. Commission on Civil Rights.

Smith, Shanna. 1990. "Testimony of Shanna L. Smith, Representative of the National Fair Housing Alliance, Inc." Hearing before the Subcommittee on Consumer and Regulatory Affairs of the Committee on Banking, Housing, and Urban Affairs of the United States Senate. In *Discrimination in Home Mortgage Lending*. Washington, D.C.: U.S. Government Printing Office.

Smith, Shanna and Cathy Cloud. 1993. "The Role of Private, Non-Profit Fair Housing Enforcement Organizations in Lending Testing." Home Mortgage Lending and Discrimination Conference, U.S. Department of Housing and Urban Development and Office of the Comptroller of the Currency, 18–19 May.

Squires, Gregory D. and William Velez. 1987. "Neighborhood Racial Composition and Mortgage Lending: City and Suburban Differences." *Journal of Urban Affairs* (23) 1: 217–32.

Squires, Gregory D., William Velez, and Karl E. Taeuber. 1991. "Insurance Redlining, Agency Location, and the Process of Urban Disinvestment." *Urban Affairs Quarterly* 26 (4): 567–88.

The Business Journal. 1992. "'Confrontational' Style Is Lending Project's Strength," 9 March.

———. 1993. "Guaranty Bank Makes $15 Million Pledge," 5 June.

Turner, Margery Austin, Raymond J. Struyk, and John Yinger. 1991. *Housing Discrimination Study.* Washington, D.C.: The Urban Institute.

Updegrave, Walter L. 1989. "Race and Money." *Money* 18 (12): 152–72.

U.S. Department of Justice. 1992. "Department of Justice Settles First Race Discrimination Lawsuit Against Major Home Mortgage Lender." News release, U.S. Department of Justice, Washington, D.C., 17 September.

U.S. Equal Employment Opportunity Commission. 1989. Unpublished data.

———. 1990. EEOC Notice no. N-915-062, 20 November.

U.S. Federal Housing Administration. 1938. *Underwriting Manual.* Washington,D.C.: U.S. Government Printing Office.

Wallace, J., W. L. Holshouser, T. S. Lane, and J. Williams. 1985. *The Fair Housing Assistance Program Evaluation.* Washington, D.C.: Office of Policy Development and Research, U.S. Department of Housing and Urban Development.

Wienk, Ronald E. 1992. "Discrimination in Urban Credit Markets: What We Don't Know and Why We Don't Know It." *Housing Policy Debate* 3 (2): 217–40.

Yinger, John. 1986. "On the Possibility of Achieving Racial Integration through Subsidized Housing." In John M. Goering (ed.), *Housing Desegregation and Federal Policy.* Chapel Hill: University of North Carolina Press.

Zarembka, Arlene. 1990. *The Urban Housing Crisis: Social, Economic, and Legal Issues and Proposals.* New York: Greenwood Press.

———. 1991. "Housing Banks." *The Nation* 252 (24): 837.

Chapter 5. Partnership and the Pursuit of the Private City

Anderson, Elijah. 1990. *Street Wise: Race, Class, and Change in an Urban Community.* Chicago: University of Chicago Press.

Aschauer, David. 1990. *Public Investment and Private Sector Growth.* Washington, D.C.: Economic Policy Institute.

Barnekov, Timothy, Robin Boyle, and Daniel Rich. 1989. *Privatism and Urban Policy in Britain and the United States.* New York: Oxford University Press.

Bennett, Larry. 1988. "Harold Washington's Chicago: Placing a Progressive City Administration in Context." *Social Policy* 19 (2): 22–28.

Bates, Douglas Joseph. 1989. "City Policy and Milwaukee's Homeless Crisis." Masters thesis, University of Wisconsin–Milwaukee.

Becker, Gary. 1986. "The Prophets of Doom have a Dismal Record." *Business Week,* 27 January, 22.

Bell, Daniel. 1960. *The End of Ideology.* New York: Free Press.

———. 1973. *The Coming of Post-Industrial Society: A Venture in Social Forecasting.* New York: Basic Books.

Bender, Thomas. 1983. "The End of the City?" *democracy* 3 (Winter): 8-20.

Binkley, Lisa and Sammis B. White. 1991. "Milwaukee 1979–1980: A Decade of Change." In *Research and Opinion.* Milwaukee: Urban Research Center, University of Wisconsin–Milwaukee.

Bluestone, Barry and Irving Bluestone. 1992. *Negotiating the Future: A Labor Perspective on American Business.* New York: Basic Books.

Bluestone, Barry and Bennett Harrison. 1982. *The Deindustrialization of America: Plant Closings, Community Abandonment, and the Dismantling of Basic Industry.* New York: Basic Books.

———. 1988. *The Great U-Turn: Corporate Restructuring and the Polarizing of America.* New York: Basic Books.

Bowles, Samuel, David M. Gordon, and Thomas E. Weisskopf. 1983. *Beyond the Waste Land: A Democratic Alternative to Economic Decline.* Garden City, N.Y.: Anchor Press/Doubleday.

———. 1990. *After the Waste Land: A Democratic Economics for the Year 2000.* New York: M. E. Sharpe.

Center for Community Change. 1989. *Bright Promises, Questionable Results: An Examination of How Well Three Government Subsidy Programs Created Jobs.* Washington, D.C.: Center for Community Change.

Chambers, Julius L. 1987. "The Law and Black Americans: Retreat From Civil Rights." In Janet Dewart (ed.), *The State of Black America 1987.* New York: The National Urban League.

Chicago Works Together: Chicago Development Plan 1984. 1984. City of Chicago.

Clavel, Pierre. 1986. *The Progressive City: Planning and Participation, 1969–1984.* New Brunswick: Rutgers University Press.

Clavel, Pierre and Nancy Kleniewski. 1990. "Space for Progressive Local Policy: Examples from the United States and the United Kingdom." In John R. Logan and Todd Swanstrom (eds.), *Beyond the City Limits: Urban Policy and Economic Restructuring in Comparative Perspective.* Philadelphia: Temple University Press.

Clavel, Pierre and Wim Wiewel (eds.). 1991. *Harold Washington and the Neighborhoods: Progressive City Government in Chicago, 1983–1987.* New Brunswick: Rutgers University Press.

Cohen, Stephen S. and John Zysman. 1987. *Manufacturing Matters: The Myth of the Post-Industrial Economy.* New York: Basic Books.

Cole, Robert E. and Donald R. Deskins, Jr. 1989. "Racial Factors in Site Location and Employment Patterns of Japanese Auto Firms." *California Management Review* 31 (1): 9–22.

Connolly, William E. 1983. "Progress, Growth, and Pessimism in America." *democracy* 3 (Fall): 22–31.

Darden, Joe, Richard Child Hill, June Thomas, and Richard Thomas. 1987. *Detroit: Race and Uneven Development.* Philadelphia: Temple University Press.

Davis, Perry. 1986. *Public-Private Partnerships: Improving Urban Life.* New York: The Academy of Political Science.

Dedman, Bill. 1989. "Blacks Turned Down for Home Loans from S&Ls Twice as Often as Whites." *The Atlanta Journal/Constitution,* 22 January.

Department of City Development. 1986. *Report of Activities 1980–1985.* City of Milwaukee.

————. 1987. *Toward Preservation Partnerships.* City of Milwaukee.

Dreier, Peter. 1989. "Economic Growth and Economic Justice in Boston: Populist Housing and Jobs Policies." In Gregory D. Squires (ed.), *Unequal Partnerships: The Political Economy of Urban Redevelopment in Postwar America.* New Brunswick: Rutgers University Press.

————. 1990. Personal communication between Peter Dreier of the Boston Redevelopment Authority and Gregory D. Squires, 6 January.

————. 1993. "America's Urban Crisis: Symptoms, Causes, Solutions." *North Carolina Law Review* 71 (5): 1351–1401.

Dreier, Peter and Bruce Ehrlich. 1991. "Downtown Development and Urban Reform: The Politics of Boston's Linkage Policy." *Urban Affairs Quarterly* 26 (3): 354–75.

Dreier, Peter and Dennis W. Keating. 1990. "The Limits of Localism: Progressive Housing Policies in Boston, 1984–1989." *Urban Affairs Quarterly* 26 (2): 191–216.

Dreier, Peter, David C. Schwartz, and Ann Greiner. 1988. "What Every Business Can Do About Housing." *Harvard Business Review* 66 (5): 52–61.

Edsall, Thomas Byrne and Mary D. Edsall. 1991. *Chain Reaction: The Impact of Race, Rights, and Taxes on American Politics.* New York: W. W. Norton.

Eisinger, Peter K. 1988. *The Rise of the Entrepreneurial State: State and Local Economic Development Policy in the United States.* Madison: University of Wisconsin Press.

Fair Lending Action Committee. 1989. "Equal Access to Mortgage Lending: The Milwaukee Plan." Report to Mayor John Norquist and Governor Tommy G. Thompson.

Feagin, Joe R. 1988. *Free Enterprise City: Houston in Political and Economic Perspective.* New Brunswick: Rutgers University Press.

————. 1991. "The Continuing Significance of Race: Antiblack Discrimination in Public Places." *American Sociological Review* 56 (1): 101–16.

Friedland, Roger. 1983. *Power and Crisis in the City: Corporations, Unions and Urban Policy.* New York: Schocken Books.

Friedman, Lawrence Meir. 1968. *Government and Slum Housing: A Century of Frustration.* Chicago: Rand McNally.

Galster, George C. and Edward W. Hill (eds.). 1992. *The Metropolis in Black & White: Place, Power and Polarization.* New Brunswick: Center for Urban Policy Research.

Garreau, Joel. 1991. *Edge City: Life on the New Frontier.* New York: Doubleday.

Giloth, Robert and John Betancur. 1988. "Where Downtown Meets Neighbor-
  hood: Industrial Displacement in Chicago, 1978–1987." *Journal of the
  American Planning Association* 54 (3): 279–90.
Goldsmith, William W. and Edward J. Blakely. 1992. *Separate Societies: Poverty
  and Inequality in U.S. Cities.* Philadelphia: Temple University Press.
Goodman, Robert. 1979. *The Last Entrepreneurs: Americas Regional Wars for Jobs
  and Dollars.* Boston: South End Press.
Govan, Reginald C. and William L. Taylor (eds.). 1989. *One Nation, Indivisible:
  The Civil Rights Challenge for the 1990s.* Washington, D.C.: Citizens Com-
  mission on Civil Rights.
Gottdiener, Mark. 1986. "Retrospect and Prospect in Urban Crisis Theory." In
  Mark Gottdiener (ed.), *Cities in Stress: A New Look at the Urban Crisis.*
  Newbury Park, Calif.: Sage Publications.
———. 1990. "Crisis Theory and State Financial Capital." *International Journal
  of Urban and Regional Research* 14 (3): 383–403.
Greider, William. 1978. "Detroit's Streetwise Mayor Plays Key Role in City's
  Turnaround." *Cleveland Plain Dealer*, 3 July. Cited in Todd Swanstrom,
  *The Crisis of Growth Politics: Cleveland, Kucinich, and the Challenge of Urban
  Populism* (Philadelphia: Temple University Press, 1985).
Harris, Fred R. and Roger W. Wilkins (eds.). 1988. *Quiet Riots: Race and Poverty
  in the United States.* New York: Pantheon Books.
Hartman, Chester. 1974. *Yerba Buena: Land Grab and Community Resistance in
  San Francisco.* San Francisco: Glide.
Hayes, Robert H. and William J. Abernathy. 1980. "Managing Our Way to Eco-
  nomic Decline." *Harvard Business Review* 58 (July / August): 67–77.
Hays, R. Allen. 1985. *The Federal Government & Urban Housing: Ideology and
  Change in Public Policy.* Albany: SUNY Press.
Jackson, Kenneth T. 1985. *Crabgrass Frontier: The Suburbanization of the United
  States.* New York: Oxford University Press.
Jacobs, Jane. 1985. *Cities and the Wealth of Nations: Principles of Economic Life.*
  New York: Vintage Books.
Jaynes, Gerald David and Robin M. Williams (eds.). 1989. *A Common Destiny:
  Blacks and American Society.* Washington, D.C.: National Academy Press.
Kain, John F. 1992. "The Spatial Mismatch Hypothesis: Three Decades Later."
  Housing Policy Debates 3 (2): 371–460.
Kasarda, John. 1988. "Economic Restructuring and America's Urban Dilemma."
  In John Kasarda and Mattei. Dogan (eds.), *A World of Giant Cities.* New-
  bury Park, Calif.: Sage Publications.
———. 1990. "Urban Employment Change and Minority Skills Mismatch." In
  Lawrence Joseph (ed.), *Creating Jobs, Creating Workers.* Chicago: Center
  for Urban Research and Policy Studies, University of Chicago.
Kirschenman, Joleen and Kathryn M. Neckerman. 1991. "'We'd Love to Hire
  Them, But . . .': The Meaning of Race for Employers." In Christopher
  Jencks and Paul E. Peterson (eds.), *The Urban Underclass.* Washington,
  D.C.: The Brookings Institution.
Krumholz, Norman. 1984. "Recovery of Cities: An Alternate View." In Paul R.
  Porter and David Sweet (eds.), *Rebuilding America's Cities: Roads to Recov-
  ery.* New Brunswick, N.J.: Center for Urban Policy Research.

Krumholz, Norman and John Forester. 1990. *Making Equity Planning Work: Leadership in the Public Sector.* Philadelphia: Temple University Press.

Langton, Stuart. 1983. "Public-Private Partnerships: Hope or Hoax?" *National Civic Review* 72 (May): 256–61.

Ledebur, Larry C. and William R. Barnes. 1992. "City Distress, Metropolitan Disparities, and Economic Growth." Washington, D.C.: National League of Cities.

Levine, Marc V. 1987. "Downtown Redevelopment as an Urban Growth Strategy: A Critical Appraisal of the Baltimore Renaissance." *Journal of Urban Affairs* 9 (2): 103–23.

———. 1989. "The Politics of Partnership: Urban Redevelopment Since 1945." In Gregory D. Squires (ed.), *Unequal Partnerships: The Political Economy of Urban Redevelopment in Postwar America.* New Brunswick: Rutgers University Press.

Levy, Frank. 1987. *Dollars and Dreams: The Changing American Income Distribution.* New York: Russell Sage Foundation.

Lindblom, Charles E. 1977. *Politics and Markets: The World's Political- Economic Systems.* New York: Basic Books.

Liss, Susan M. and William L. Taylor (eds.). 1991. *Lost Opportunities: The Civil Rights Record of the Bush Administrtion Mid-Term.* Washington, D.C.: Citizens Commission on Civil Rights.

Logan, John R. and Harvey L. Molotch. 1987. *Urban Fortunes: The Political Economy of Place.* Berkeley: University of California Press.

Marchetti, Peter. 1980. "Runaways and Takeovers: Their Effect on Milwaukee's Economy." *Urbanism Past and Present* 5 (2): 1–11.

Marchione, Marilynn. 1990. "As It Developed, '89 Was Very Good Year." *Milwaukee Journal,* 2 January.

Marshall, Ray and Marc Tucker. 1992. *Thinking for a Living: Education and the Wealth of Nations.* New York: Basic Books.

Massey, Douglas S. and Nancy A. Denton. 1993. *American Apartheid: Segregation and the Making of the Underclass.* Cambridge, Mass.: Harvard University Press.

McKenzie, Richard. 1979. *Restrictions on Business Mobility: A Study in Political Rhetoric and Economic Reality.* Washington, D.C.: American Enterprise Institute.

McNeely, R. L. and M. R. Kinlow. 1987. *Milwaukee Today: A Racial Gap Study.* Milwaukee: The Milwaukee Urban League.

Mier, Robert. 1989. "Neighborhood and Region: An Experiential Basis for Understanding." *Economic Development Quarterly* 3 (2): 169–74.

———. 1993. *Social Justice and Local Development Policy.* Newbury Park, Calif.: Sage Publications.

Mier, Robert, Kari J. Moe, and Irene Sherr. 1986. "Strategic Planning and the Pursuit of Reform, Economic Development, and Equity." *Journal of the American Planning Association* 52 (3): 299–309.

Milwaukee Journal. 1990. "The State's Bloodiest Year Ever," 2 January.

Mishel, Lawrence and Jacqueline Simon. 1988. *The State of Working America.* Washington, D.C.: Economic Policy Institute.

Norman, Jack. 1989. "Congenial Milwaukee: A Segregated City." In Gregory D. Squires (ed.), *Unequal Partnerships: The Political Economy of Urban Redevelopment in Postwar America*. New Brunswick: Rutgers University Press.

Nyden, Philip W. and Wim Wiewel (eds.). 1991. *Challenging Uneven Development: An Urban Agenda for the 1990s*. New Brunswick: Rutgers University Press.

Orfield, Gary. 1988. "Separate Societies: Have the Kerner Warnings Come True?" In Fred R. Harris and Roger W. Wilkins (eds.), *Quiet Riots: Race and Poverty in the United States*. New York: Pantheon Books.

Osborne, David and Ted Gaebler. 1992. *Reinventing Government*. Reading, Mass.: Addison-Wesley.

Page, Clarence. 1987. Personal interview with Gregory D. Squires, 19 March.

Persky, Joseph, Elliott Sclar, and Wim Wiewel. 1991. *Does America Need Cities? An Urban Investment Strategy for National Prosperity*. Washington, D.C.: Economic Policy Institute.

Peterson, George and Carol Lewis (eds.). 1986. *Reagan and the Cities*. Washington, D.C.: The Urban Institute.

Peterson, Paul E. 1981. *City Limits*. Chicago: University of Chicago Press.

———— (ed.). 1985. *The New Urban Reality*. Washington, D.C.: The Brookings Institution.

Porter, Douglas R. 1989. "Balancing the Interests in Public/Private Partnerships." *Urban Land* 48 (5): 36–37.

President's Commission for a National Agenda for the Eighties. 1980. *A National Agenda for the Eighties*. Washington, D.C.: U.S. Government Printing Office.

Reich, Robert B. 1983. *The Next American Frontier*. New York: Times Books.

————. 1987. *Tales of a New America*. New York: Times Books.

————. 1991. *The Work of Nations*. New York: Vintage Books.

Savitch, H. V. et al. Undated. "Ties That Bind: Central Cities, Suburbs and the New Metropolitan Region." School of Urban Policy. University of Louisville. Cited in Peter Dreier, "America's Urban Crisis: Symptoms, Causes, Solutions." *North Carolina Law Review* 71 (5).

Sbragia, Alberta. 1989. "The Pittsburgh Model of Economic Development: Partnership, Responsiveness, and Indifference." In Gregory D. Squires (ed.), *Unequal Partnerships: The Political Economy of Urban Redevelopment in Postwar America*. New Brunswick: Rutgers University Press.

Schmidt, William. 1987. "U.S. Downtowns: No Longer Downtrodden." *New York Times*, 11 October.

Schneider, William. 1992. "The Suburban Century Begins." *The Atlantic* 270 (1): 33–44.

Schumpeter, Joseph. 1942. *Capitalism, Socialism, and Democracy*. New York: Harper and Row.

Schwarz, John E. and Thomas J. Volgy. 1992. *The Forgotten Americans*. New York: W. W. Norton.

Shearer, Derek. 1989. "In Search of Equal Partnerships: Prospects for Progressive Urban Policy in the 1990s." In Gregory D. Squires (ed.), *Unequal Partnerships: The Political Economy of Urban Redevelopment in Postwar America*. New Brunswick: Rutgers University Press.

Smith, Michael Peter and Dennis R. Judd. 1984. "American Cities: The Production of Ideology." In Michael Peter Smith and Dennis R. Judd (eds.), *Cities in Transformation: Class, Capital, and the State*. Beverly Hills: Sage Publications.

Southeastern Wisconsin Regional Planning Commission. 1989. Data provided in letter from Kurt W. Bauer, Executive Director, 9 November.

Squires, Gregory D. 1984. "Capital Mobility versus Upward Mobility: The Racially Discriminatory Consequences of Plant Closings and Corporate Relocations." In Larry Sawers and William K. Tabb (eds.), *Sunbelt/Snowbelt: Urban Development and Regional Restructuring*. New York: Oxford University Press.

———— (ed.). 1989. *Unequal Partnerships: The Political Economy of Urban Redevelopment in Postwar America*. New Brunswick: Rutgers University Press.

Squires, Gregory D., Larry Bennett, Kathleen McCourt, and Philip Nyden. 1987. *Chicago: Race, Class, and the Response to Urban Decline*. Philadelphia: Temple University Press.

Squires, Gregory D. and William Velez. 1987. "Insurance Redlining and the Transformation of an Urban Metropolis." *Urban Affairs Quarterly* 23 (1): 63–83.

Stone, Clarence N. 1987. "The Study of the Politics of Urban Development." In Clarence N. Stone and Heywood T. Sanders (eds.), *The Politics of Urban Development*. Lawrence: University of Kansas Press.

Stuart, Reginald. 1983. "Business Said to Have Barred New Plants in Largely Black Communities." *New York Times*, 15 February.

Taylor, William L. 1989. "Special Report: Supreme Court Decisions do Grave Damage to Equal Employment Opportunity Law." *Civil Rights Monitor* 4 (2): 1–28.

Teaford, Jon C. 1990. *The Rough Road to Renaissance: Urban Revitalization in America, 1940–1985*. Baltimore: Johns Hopkins University Press.

Thomas, June Manning. 1989. "Detroit: The Centrifugal City." In Gregory D. Squires (ed.), *Unequal Partnerships: The Political Economy of Urban Redevelopment in Postwar America*. New Brunswick: Rutgers University Press.

Thurow, Lester. 1992. *Head to Head: The Coming Economic Battle among Japan, Europe, and America*. New York: William Morrow & Company.

Tisdale, William. 1992. Personal communication with Gregory D. Squires, 20 November.

Turner, Margery and Michael Fix. 1991. *Opportunities Denied, Opportunities Diminished*. Washington, D.C.: The Urban Institute.

Updegrave, Walter L. 1989. "Race and Money." *Money* 18 (12): 152–72.

Urban Institute. 1992. "Confronting the Nation's Urban Crisis." *The Urban Institute Policy and Research Report* 22 (2): 1–3.

U.S. Bureau of the Census. 1976. *The Statistical History of the United States: From Colonial Times to the Present*. New York: Basic Books.

————. 1980. *Structural Equipment and Household Characteristics of Housing Units*, table H7. Washington, D.C.: U.S. Government Printing Documents.

————. 1989. *Statistical Abstract of the United States 1989*. Washington, D.C.: U.S. Government Printing Office.

————. 1992. *Statistical Abstract of the United States 1992*. Washington, D.C.: U.S. Government Printing Office.

Warner, Sam Bass, Jr. 1987. *The Private City: Philadelphia in Three Periods of Its Growth*. Philadelphia: University of Pennsylvania Press.

West, Cornel. 1993. *Race Matters*. Boston: Beacon Press.

White, Sammis B., Peter D. Reynolds, William McMahon, and James Paetsch. 1989. "City and Suburban Impacts of Industrial Change in Milwaukee, 1979–87." The Urban Research Center, University of Wisconsin–Milwaukee.

Wilberg, Janice and Mark G. Wojno. 1992. "Expected to Work But No Jobs: Job Availability in Milwaukee." Milwaukee: Social Development Commission.

Wilson, William J. 1987. *The Truly Disadvantaged: The Inner City, the Underclass, and Public Policy*. Chicago: University of Chicago Press.

Ziehlsdorf et al. versus American Family Insurance Group. 1988. Case no. 88CV1082, Waukesha County Circuit Court.

Chapter 6. Toward a More Livable City

Baran, Paul A. 1961. "The Commitment of the Intellectual." *Monthly Review* 13: 8–18.

Bellah, Robert N., Richard Madsen, William M. Sullivan, Ann Swidler, and Steven M. Tipton. 1985. *Habits of the Heart: Individualism and Commitment in American Life*. Berkeley: University of California Press.

Branch, Taylor. 1989. *Parting the Waters: America in the King Years*. New York: Touchstone.

Brody, David. 1980. *Workers in Industrial America*. New York: Oxford University Press.

Freeman, Alan. 1988. "Racism, Rights and the Quest for Equality of Opportunity: A Critical Legal Essay." *Harvard Civil Rights-Civil Liberties Law Review* 23: 295–392.

Freeman, Richard B. and James L. Medoff. 1984. *What Do Unions Do?* New York: Basic Books.

Green, James (ed.). 1983. *Workers' Struggles, Past and Present: A "Radical America" Reader*. Philadelphia: Temple University Press.

Lynd, Robert S. 1939. *Knowledge for What? The Place of Social Science in American Culture*. Princeton: Princeton University Press.

Morris, Aldon D. 1984. *The Origins of the Civil Rights Movement*. New York: The Free Press.

Osborne, David. 1988. *Laboratories of Democracy*. Boston: Harvard Business School Press.

Rothstein, Richard. 1993. "Unions and the New Administration." *Dissent* (Spring): 159–65.

Tawney, R. H. 1964. *Equality*. London: George Allen and Unwin.

Weisbrot, Robert. 1990. *Freedom Bound: A History of America's Civil Rights Movement*. New York: W. W. Norton Co.

Index

/307.34b5774C>Cl/

DATE DUE